Archdioce
and Dioce
of Irelan
2000

GW00686134

VERITAS

2000

Published 2000 by
Veritas Publications
7-8 Lower Abbey Street
Dublin 1

Copyright © Irish Catholic Bishops' Conference, 2000

ISBN 1 85390 580 1

Designed by Bill Bolger
Origination by Accuplate Ltd, Dublin
Printed in the Republic of Ireland by Criterion Press Ltd, Dublin

This publication has
been supported by the
generous sponsorship
of

Church & General
A company of the Allianz Group ©

Contents

Archdiocese of Armagh

Most Rev Seán Brady DCL, DD

Dr Brady, a native of Laragh, Co Cavan, Diocese of Kilmore, was born in August 1939. He was educated at Caulfield National School, Laragh, St Patrick's College, Cavan, St Patrick's College, Maynooth, and the Irish College, Rome, where he was ordained in February 1964. He received a Doctorate in Canon Law at the Lateran University in 1967.

His first appointment was as professor in St Patrick's College, Cavan, from 1967 to 1980. In 1980 he was appointed Vice-Rector of the Irish College, Rome, and in 1987 he became Rector of the College, a post he held until 1993, when he returned to Ireland to become Parish Priest of Castletara, Co Cavan (Ballyhaise). On 19 February 1995 he was ordained Coadjutor Archbishop of Armagh, and on the retirement of Cardinal Cahal B. Daly, he succeeded as Archbishop of Armagh and Primate of All Ireland on 1 October 1996. He was installed as Archbishop of Armagh on 3 November 1996.

Archbishop Brady is Chairman of the Irish Episcopal Conference.

St Patrick's Cathedral, Armagh

The building of the new St Patrick's Cathedral lasted from St Patrick's Day 1840, when the foundation stone was laid, until its solemn consecration in 1904. There were occasional intermissions of the work, and one of the longest gaps occurred because of the Great Famine. Primate Crolly, who had initiated the building, became a victim of famine cholera, and, at his own wish, his body was laid to rest under the sanctuary of the unfinished cathedral.

For five years the low outline of the bare walls remained, but with the translation of Dr Paul Cullen to the See of Dublin, work was resumed under Primate Dixon. On Easter Monday 1854, tarpaulins and canvas covers were drawn from wall to wall to allow Mass to be celebrated in the unfinished building.

One consequence of the Famine cessation was that the original architect, Thomas J. Duff, was dead. The architect to take over from Duff's original Perpendicular Gothic design was J. J. McCarthy, destined to become one of the famous architects of the nineteenth century. In his anxiety to achieve a greater degree of classical purity, McCarthy drew up a continuation design in the old fourteenth-century Decorated Gothic. While critics may debate the wisdom of such a radical change when the building had reached a relatively advanced stage, the effect was undoubtedly to create an overall impression of massive grandeur.

The final impetus to complete the building came when Dr McGettigan was appointed (1870) to Armagh, and the solemn dedication took place in 1873.

Dr Logue, following Primate McGettigan's death, was to achieve the splendid interior decoration and the addition of the Synod Hall. He travelled to Rome and Carrara in search of precious marble for the reredos, pulpit and altar, and it was he also who achieved the decoration of the interior

with mosaic. Under him, stained-glass windows were commissioned from Meyer in Germany. Cardinal Vanutelli represented Pope Pius X at the solemn consecration in 1904. A grand carillon was installed in 1924.

Vatican II's decree on Sacred Liturgy stressed the participation of the laity and hence greater visibility had to be afforded to the congregation. For this reason all the architects who submitted designs based their plans on the removal of the 1904 marble screens, which hindered visibility of the sanctuary from the sides. By raising, enlarging and opening the sanctuary area, the cathedral has, to a large extent, been restored to its original form.

With the removal of the rood screen, a new crucifix had to be placed at the sanctuary, and a specially commissioned 'Cross of Life' by Imogen Stuart was affixed to the right of the sanctuary.

The rededication took place in 1982, and a portion of St Malachy's relics from France, together with a relic of St Oliver Plunkett, was placed in the new altar. And so, the mortal remains of two of Armagh's most celebrated *comharbaí Phádraig* were carried back to the scene of their labours in more troubled times.

A unique, but now also an historical feature of the primatial cathedral, is the Cardinals' Hats. They are no longer conferred on new Cardinals. They were hung here and went deliberately untended so that their decay would represent the end of all earthly glory. The most recently hung (and last to be presented) is that of Cardinal Conway. Beside it are Cardinal Logue's and Cardinal O'Donnell's, while on the opposite side are the hats of Cardinals D'Alton and MacRory.

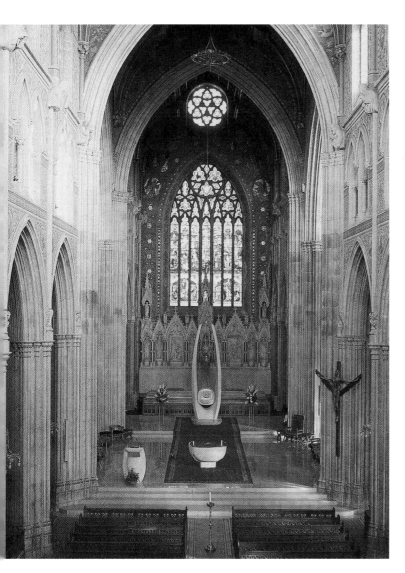

Armagh

Lady Altar Reredos

This fine specimen of Irish carving is almost the sole remnant of the old decorations that has been deemed worthy to retain its place amid modern renovation.

Its lower portion consists of an arcade of deeply recessed niches and panels, nine in all, separated by double-clustered columns of the old marble of Armagh and Down. The central niche immediately over the tabernacle contains a decorated figure of the Madonna and Child, the gift of the Christian Doctrine Society of Armagh. On each side, in niches, are the parents of the Blessed Virgin Mary, on the Gospel side St Joachim with the Temple offering of the poor, a pair of doves in a cage, and, on the Epistle side, St Anne with open book displaying the famous prophecy of Isais, '*Ecce Biego concipiet, et pariet filium*' ('Behold a Virgin shall conceive and bear a son'). Outside these are two sculptured panels in bas-relief, the Annunciation being the subject of the Gospel side, and the Nativity of our Lord on the Epistle side. Next come two niches containing figures of St Patrick (Epistle side) and St Malachy (Gospel side) with the pallium, and in his hand the saint's traditional symbol, the apple.

The two extreme end niches contain statutes of St Peter with the Keys and St Paul with the sword with which he was beheaded.

Archdiocese of
Armagh

HISTORY OF THE DIOCESE

FOUNDED BY St Patrick in the mid fifth century, the Church in Armagh soon developed on native monastic lines, with abbots who were at first also bishops, but later, rarely so. To its school flocked students, native and foreign. Its pre-eminence among Irish ecclesiastical foundations is attested in documents from 640 on.

Despite a new Culdee foundation in the eighth century, which survived until the sixteenth, Armagh's religious and scholarly attainments declined in the ninth and tenth centuries in the face of Danish raids and local warfare. The way was thus opened for the intrusion of lay abbots, and a powerful local family, the Clann Sinaigh, held the abbacy from 965 until 1129. One of its members, Ceallach (St Celsus), ended the abuse by having himself ordained bishop in 1106.

At the Synod of Rathbreasail, 1111, the territory assigned to each Irish see was outlined and Armagh received almost the whole of its present territory.

Before Ceallach's death in 1129 he chose as his successor (St) Malachy. In the face of stern opposition from Clann Sinaigh, who were unwilling to recognise an archbishop not belonging to their family, Malachy resigned his see. Gelasius (1137-74) received the pallium at the Synod of Kells, 1152. Conchubhar Mac Conchaille (1174-75) is still venerated as St Concord – the French finding his Irish name difficult to pronounce – for his sanctity at Chambery, where he died on his return journey from Rome.

The Anglo-Norman invasion brought a see-saw struggle between Irish and Anglo-Irish for possession of the see and it also prepared the way for conflicts with Dublin over the primacy. Maolpádraig Ó Scanlan (1261-70) erected a larger cathedral, of which the present Church of Ireland cathedral is an eighteenth-century rebuilding. Nicholas MacMaoliosa (1272-1303) was the last archbishop of Irish race until the Reformation. The most noteworthy

Norman primate was Richard Fitz-Ralph (1346-60), famous for his contests with the Mendicant Orders. The diocese was virtually partitioned into Armagh *inter Hibernicos* (Cos Armagh, Tyrone and Derry) and Armagh *inter Anglos* (Co Louth). One of Milo Sweetman's (1361-80) constitutions made it obligatory for all bishops to work for peace between Irish and Anglo-Irish, with excommunication for any bishop who sowed discord between the two nations. The Arch-bishops of Armagh, both as custodians of the peace in Co Louth and as mediators among the conflicting camps, performed a vital service in the maintenance of public order on the Irish march. They provided a framework for Christians that bridged the gulf between the two 'nations'. The archbishops resided in their manors at Dromiskin and Termonfeckin and left the northern portion of the diocese to be administered by the dean – normally of Irish race. At the Reformation, Primates George Cromer (1521) and George Dowdall (1553-58), though they strongly opposed doctrinal changes, failed to provide the intrepid leadership of their successors.

Outstanding among the Post-Reformation primates were Richard Creagh (1564-85), who spent eighteen years before his death in the Tower of London; Hugh O'Reilly (1628-53), who played a prominent part in the Confederation of Kilkenny; Edmund O'Reilly (1657-69); Oliver Plunkett (1669-81) and Hugh McMahon (1714-37). The latter's *Jus Primatiale Armacanum* virtually settled the long-standing dispute with Dublin over the primacy. Archbishops Peter Lombard (1601-25) and Hugh MacCawell (1626) were distinguished scholars who spent their lives in exile. Despite the Penal Laws, Armagh still had twenty-five mass houses, served by seventy-six diocesan priests and twenty-two friars, in 1731.

The gradual easing of the Penal Laws in the second half of the eighteenth century allowed many small churches to be built. Discipline, which had by now become slack, was restored by Richard Reilly (1787-1818). William Crolly (1835-49) took up residence in

Armagh – after an absence of centuries – and began the erection of St Patrick's Cathedral (foundation 17 March 1840). He also built the diocesan seminary (1838), and during his time at least fifteen churches were built, some of them with Protestant support. Under Joseph Dixon (1852-66) the Diocesan Chapter was re-constituted. Daniel McGettigan (1870-87) and his two immediate successors were all translated from Raphoe. The building of the cathedral was completed and dedicated (1873) by Dr McGettigan, who also buil the primate's residence 'Ara Coeli' (1876-77). Michael Logue (1887-1924) commissioned and had completed the splendid interior decoration of the cathedral and it was consecrated in 1904 Archbishop Logue was the first occupan of the see to be made Cardinal (1893), and his successors, Patrick O'Donnell (1925), Joseph MacRory (1929), John D'Alton (1953), William Conway (1965) Tomás Ó Fiaich (1979) and Cahal B. Daly (1991) have been created Cardinals

The nineteenth century witnessed a phenomenal growth in organised religious life in Ireland, and Religious played a vital role in areas such as education and nursing. The Vincentian Fathers conducted St Patrick's College from 1861 to 1988 and the Nazareth Sisters were in Portadown up to the end of 1985. Tribute goes to the Mendicant Orders for their steadfastness to the faith through dark and oppressive centuries.

From a Parliamentary Return of 183 we know that Mass was still being celebrated on Sundays and holy days 'at an altar in the open air' at nine Mass stations in the northern end of the diocese. Diocesan Returns in 1864 show that from 1800 to 1864, ninety-three new churches were built, and there was an increase of eighteen priests and seven religious communities.

The Second Vatican Council necessitated many alterations in churches, to involve 'the full, conscious and active participation of all the faithful'. The newly designed cathedral sanctuary was dedicated in June 1982. Some nineteen new churches have also been erected.

Among many diocesan Post-Conciliar initiatives were the opening of Mount Oliver Pastoral Institute (1969); the Diocesan Assembly of Priests (1981); the Diocesan Mission to Lagos (1982); and the appointment of a diocesan Director of Ecumenism.

The events in recent years of special significance to the diocese were the canonisation of St Oliver Plunkett (1975), the beatification of Tyrone-born Father Patrick Loughran (1992), and the appointment and episcopal ordination (1977) of the first Armachian since St Malachy. The sudden and dramatic circumstances of Cardinal Ó Fiaich's death were lamented nationwide, but especially in his native see. After six years as 113th Comharba Phádraig, Cardinal Cahal B. Daly announced his resignation. His leadership was a bright beacon in dark days. On the feast day of St Malachy, 1996, Dr Seán Brady, the fourth priest from the diocese of Kilmore to do so, became the 114th Comharba Phádraig.

Ireland rejoiced as never before during the visit of Pope John Paul II to our native land in September 1979. This brief outline is concluded with the words of the Pope's address at Drogheda: 'Faith and fidelity are the marks of the Church in Ireland.... These are the historical signs marking the track of faith on Irish soil.... The See of Armagh, the See of Patrick, is the place to see that track, to feel these roots.'

PLACE OF PILGRIMAGE

Faughart – An Ancient Irish Pilgrimage Shrine

Faughart has been designated the Millennium Place of Pilgrimage for the Archdiocese of Armagh. Devotion to St Brigid, one of our national patrons, is of ancient origin and would seem to have begun during her lifetime. Brigid's cult grew to a status second only to that of Patrick, and to the Irish she was known as Mary of the Gael.

According to tradition, Brigid was born at Fochard Muirtheimne, a few miles north of Dundalk about AD 450. Because of the strength of this tradition, the place was later known as Fochard Bríde.

It is believed that Brigid spent her early years in this scenic area of north Co Louth, and the ancient penitential 'stations' linked with St Brigid's Stream have been performed here from ancient times. The original shrine remained largely in a primitive condition until the early 1930s, when the present shrine was erected by local labour and a national pilgrimage organised.

On the first Sunday in July 1934, an estimated 10,000 to 15,000 assembled at Faughart. This great congregation included the head of the Government, several Ministers of State, the Lord Mayor of Dublin, and several members of Dublin Corporation.

Today pilgrims visit Fochard Bríde daily. Public pilgrimages are held during the year, a candlelight procession takes place on the saint's feastday (1 February), a Mass for the Sick is celebrated in early June and there is a national pilgrimage on the first weekend in July. At public pilgrimages the pilgrims are blessed with the relic of the saint, preserved under the altar in the nearby Church of St Brigid at Kilcurry. Many remarkable graces and temporal favours have been claimed as outcome of the pilgrimage to Faughart.

Archdiocese of Dublin

Most Rev Desmond Connell DD

Born in Dublin in March 1926, Desmond Connell received his early education at St Peter's primary school, Phibsboro, and at Belvedere College, before attending University College Dublin (1943-47), where he obtained a BA and MA. He was ordained a priest in March 1951 and then spent two years at the Catholic University of Louvain, where he obtained a D. Phil.

On his return to Ireland in 1953 he was appointed Assistant Lecturer at UCD, where he remained in various posts until 1988: College Lecturer from 1963 to 1972, Professor of General Metaphysics and Head of the Department of Metaphysics from 1972 to 1988, and Dean of the Faculty of Philosophy from 1984 to 1988.

He was ordained Archbishop of Dublin and Primate of Ireland on 6 March 1988.

Dr Connell is the author of several books and has contributed widely to philosophical and theological reviews. He was made Prelate of Honour in 1984 and awarded a D. Litt for published work by the National University of Ireland in 1981.

He is Vice-President of the Irish Episcopal Conference; Chairman of the Episcopal Commission for Doctrine, of the Theological Commission, and of the Episcopal Commission for Universities; a member of the Episcopal Commission on Ecumenism, of the Committee for European Affairs, and of the Inter-Church Committee; a member of the Congregation for the Doctrine of the Faith, of the Pontifical Council for the Pastoral Care of Migrants and Itinerant People and of the Congregation for Bishops.

St Mary's Pro-Cathedral, Dublin

Though Catholic Dublin has not possessed a cathedral since the Reformation, for almost two hundred years now St Mary's Pro-Cathedral has served as the Mother Church of the Dublin arch-diocese. In that time it has won a special place in the hearts of the Dublin people, to whom it is known affectionately as 'The Pro'.

The Pro-Cathedral was born of the vision of Archbishop John Thomas Troy and brought to fruition thanks to the unstinting labours of its second administrator, Archdeacon John Hamilton. The parish of Saint Mary's, straddling the Liffey, was established in 1707 and a chapel dedicated to St Mary was opened in 1729. In 1797 Archbishop Troy successfully petitioned the Holy See to allow him take St Mary's as his *mensa* parish. He thereupon set about raising funds to build a 'dignified, spacious church' in a central location in the parish.

The site chosen was a building on Marlborough Street, opposite Tyrone House. Formerly the town house of the Earl of Annesley, it was purchased for £5,100 and a deposit was paid in 1803. However, it was not until 1814 that designs were publicly invited for the new church. A design of uncertain authorship, marked only with the letter 'P', for a church in the form of a Grecian Doric temple, was chosen as the winner. The only substantial alteration to the design was the erection of a dome.

The foundation stone was laid by Archbishop Troy in 1815. On the feast of St Laurence O'Toole in 1825, Archbishop Murray celebrated High Mass, to mark the dedication of the church to the 'Conception of the Virgin Mary', to a packed congregation, which included Daniel O'Connell. After the dedication the interior embellishment of the church continued. Highlights included the alto relief representation of the Ascension by John Smyth; the high altar carved by Peter Turnerelli, and the marble statues

Our Lady of Dublin

The life-size black oak statue of Our Lady with Child was venerated originally in the Cistercian Abbey, Mary Street. Rescued from Cromwellian forces when the abbey was surrendered, it was secretly preserved for posterity. Found by Fr John Spratt OCarm in 1824, it has been in Whitefriar Street ever since. Its survival is symbolic of tenacious faith in difficult times.

Archbishops Murray and Cullen by Thomas Farrell. Stained-glass windows, depicting Our Lady flanked by St Laurence O'Toole and St Kevin, were installed behind the sanctuary in 1886.

The high point of liturgical embellishment was the generous benefaction by Edward Martyn, who endowed the Palestrina choir for male voices in 1902.

Archdiocese of Dublin

HISTORY OF THE DIOCESE

THE ARCHDIOCESE of Dublin covers all of Co Dublin, nearly all of Co Wicklow, with much of Co Kildare and fragments of Cos Carlow, Wexford and Laois. This area was Christian long before Dublin had a diocese, and the remains and memory of monasteries famous before that time, at Glendalough, Rathmichael, Tallaght and Kilnamanagh, among others, are witness to the faith of earlier generations, and to a flourishing Church life in their time.

The Norse of the kingdom of Dublin first sought to have a bishop of their own in the eleventh century, and they sent their chosen candidate to be consecrated in Canterbury. They obviously wanted to keep some distance from the Irish around them, and through trading contacts were interested in how things were done in England. This isolation ended when Dublin was made an archdiocese in 1152, and the second archbishop was St Laurence O'Toole, previously Abbot of Glendalough.

St Laurence's lifetime saw many changes in Ireland. Religious orders from the Continent came here, and Laurence installed a community of canons to minister in the Cathedral of Holy Trinity, later known as Christchurch. The Abbey of St Mary was founded in Dublin at that time, first Benedictine, then Cistercian, which for several centuries was to be an important religious centre for Dublin and its surroundings.

Not only was the Irish Church transformed in the twelfth century by new organisation and new arrivals from abroad, but Ireland's political scene was changed permanently by the coming of the Normans. St Laurence's successor was a Norman, and from then onward to the time of the Reformation, Dublin's archbishops were all either Norman or English. It was the medieval pattern of things. High offices in the Church were never free of political influence, and in fact many of Dublin's archbishops exercised civil authority for the English

crown. Archbishop Henry's name appears in the text of the Magna Charta, along with the names of English bishops as witnesses. With the intention of strengthening the diocese, approval was obtained from Pope Innocent III to unite the Diocese of Glendalough with Dublin in 1216. The faith flourished too. Augustinians, Dominicans, Franciscans and Carmelites had houses in Dublin. The great convent of Grace Dieu, near Donabate, was an example of women's religious life and education.

Medieval parish churches can be traced outside the city and towns. Tully, which dated from very ancient times, Kilgobbin, Kill of the Grange, Kilbarrack and Howth are examples. Today their ruined walls seem small to modern eyes, but the population was sparse in those days, and simple buildings were adequate, many roofed with thatch. Dublin acquired a second cathedral, Saint Patrick's, built outside the city walls by an archbishop anxious to keep his freedom of action from the city's governor. In addition to his palace of St Sepulchre (where Kevin Street Garda Station is today) the archbishop had his castle at Swords, and the Abbot of St Mary's Abbey had his castle, too, at Bulloch Harbour near Dalkey, where he levied customs duties on all goods in what was then a busy commercial port.

Medieval times saw many pilgrimages. In addition to Glendalough, pilgrimages were made regularly to Our Lady's Shrine at Trim, in Meath, and overseas to the great shrine of St James, at Compostella in Spain, assembling at St James' Church and leaving the city by St James' Gate, as was the custom in other European cities as well.

The Reformation in the sixteenth century brought suffering and death. Churches and church buildings were lost, and when not destroyed they became centres of foreign influence and colonising power. Dublin had its martyrs, such as Blessed Francis Taylor, mayor of the city, Blessed Margaret Bermingham – Mrs Ball, and Archbishop Peter Talbot, who died in prison for the faith. Others from outside Dublin were martyred here for the faith, such as Blessed Dermot O'Hurley, Archbishop of Cashel, who is

buried in the little churchyard of St Kevin's, off Camden Street, Blessed Conor O'Devaney, Bishop of Down an Conor, and Blessed Patrick O'Loughran a priest of Co Tyrone. These deaths for the faith made a great impression on Dublin's people, and strengthened their attachment to the faith of their ancestor for generations to come.

As persecution eased, little Mass houses were opened here and there, usually off the beaten track. Some that have since entirely disappeared are marked on maps as far back as the eighteenth century, and the memory of Mass paths in certain country places has lasted until today. The buildings were the simplest, of mud walls and thatch roofs, with the most primitive of furnishings. The same tale was repeated all over Ireland. The King born in a stable held court in a shack.

The eighteenth and nineteenth centuries were a time of reconstruction and revival, after the winter of persecution. In the 1770s and 1780s Archbishop Carpenter issued instructions about prayers to be said in the diocese in Irish and English. Both languages were in common use among ordinary people. The 1800s saw the grea work of the new Religious congregation Mary Aikenhead with the Sisters of Charity, Catherine McAuley with her House of Mercy in Baggot Street, Margaret Aylward with the Holy Faith Sisters, Blessed Edmund Rice from Waterford with O'Connell Schools in Richmond Street and the School in Hannover Street, which later moved to Westland Row. Daniel O'Connell was the leader of many initiatives to regain Catholic freedom of worship. In these years Archbishop Daniel Murray was th wise guide of all this work of renewal. I Murray played a special role when the Loreto Sisters, the Irish branch of the Institute of the Blessed Virgin Mary, w founded by his devoted friend Mother Frances ('Fanny') Ball. A name associated with so much suffering for th faith came back three centuries later to rejoice in its restoration.

The restoration of Catholic education led to missionary work. The Jesuits at the

Catholic University and at Milltown Park, the Holy Ghost Fathers at Kimmage Manor and Blackrock must be remembered among many others. Two outstanding archbishops must be mentioned, to stand for many: Paul Cullen, who became Ireland's first Cardinal in 1866, and Dr McQuaid in the present century, both men of real greatness. Increase of population to more than a million Catholics has brought a doubling of Dublin's parishes in the last fifty years, to reach the present total of 200.

PLACE OF PILGRIMAGE

Glendalough – A Sacred Place of Healing and Peace

Glendalough, once a thriving centre of Celtic Christian spirituality, is the central place of pilgrimage in the archdiocese of Dublin and one of the great pilgrim places of Europe. Often referred to as the 'Valley of the Two Lakes', it is known, not only to thousands of Irish people, but to people from all over the world who come as tourists and pilgrims to spend time among its mountains, lakes and sacred ruins.

Although there are structures in the valley that may be from pre-Christian times, the history of Glendalough begins with St Kevin. Over 1400 years ago, he renounced a life of privilege and came to live as a hermit in a cave in Glendalough.

As disciples joined him, the monastery was founded, and Glendalough became a great centre of spirituality and learning, which flourished for over 600 years, up to the time of the Norman invasion. Both patrons of the Dublin diocese lived in Glendalough: while St Kevin (Caoimhín) was the founding figure, St Laurence (Lorcán) O'Toole spent time here as a monk and later nine years as Abbot of Glendalough before becoming Archbishop of Dublin in 1162. The ancient Diocese of Glendalough was incorporated into the Archdiocese of Dublin in 1216.

Over the centuries that followed, Glendalough was destroyed by fire and sacked many times. Valuable manuscripts were lost in these catastrophes. Whatever was left of the monastery was suppressed at the time of the Reformation and very little is known of Glendalough during the sixteenth, seventeenth and eighteenth centuries, but it seems clear that some form of pilgrimage to the sacred site continued

even in those times of penal repression of the Catholic faith.

Glendalough was rediscovered in the late eighteenth century by antiquaries and artists. In 1869 the monastic site was vested in the Commission of Public Works, and in the late nineteenth century the Office of Public Works made detailed descriptions of the ruins and carried out very valuable restoration work on some of the buildings. This site is now vested in Dúchas, the Heritage Service.

Glendalough's Landmarks: The ruins that can be seen in Glendalough today are concentrated in two areas. The remains of the Monastic City lie at the eastern end of the valley and include the Cathedral, St Kevin's Church, St Kieran's Church, the Priest's House and Cemetery, St Kevin's Cross and the Round Tower. Trinity Church and St Mary's Church are nearby, while St Saviour's Church and St Kevin's Well lie a little farther along the valley to the east. The earlier ruins straddle the shores of the Upper Lake – in the area known as 'St Kevin's Desert'. There we find St Kevin's Cell, Reefert Church, Teampaill na Sceillig, which is believed to be the oldest church in Glendalough, and St Kevin's Bed in the rock face above the Upper Lake, where St Kevin and St Laurence are known to have spent long periods alone in prayer – especially during the penitential seasons. The Green Road along the foot of

Derrybawn Mountain links the two ends of the valley.

Glendalough Parish Today: The valley of Glendalough and the surrounding districts still continue to be home for many Christians. There are both Church of Ireland and Catholic communities in the area. The Catholic Parish Church of St Kevin is located just three miles from the Monastic City at Brockagh, near the village of Laragh. Built between 1841 and 1851 by a people experiencing the hardships of famine Ireland, this place of prayer represents an integrated continuation of the spiritual richness of Glendalough. The church now enshrines two newly commissioned icons of St Kevin and St Laurence O'Toole and is now also the focus of a diocesan initiative to celebrate the Great Jubilee of AD 2000.

Glendalough 2000 'Suaimhneas Chaoimhín' will include:
* restoration of the unique Parish Church of St Kevin;
* provision of retreat facilities;
* five *cillíns* – simple accommodation units in keeping with tradition;
* *séipéal beag*;
* establishment of a Meditation Garden;
* extended facilities for young people.
These will be situated within the grounds of the parish church.

Archdiocese of
Cashel and Diocese of Emly

Most Rev Dermot Clifford MSc,
PhD, DD

Dermot Clifford was born in Rathanny,
Ballymacellitott, on 25 January 1939. He
was educated at Clogher National School
and St Brendan's College, Killarney.
Among his teachers at St Brendan's was
the late Bishop of Kerry, Dr Diarmaid
Ó Súilleabháin.

From Killarney, he moved to St Patrick's
College, Maynooth, where he graduated
with a BSc Degree in 1960. After
Maynooth, he went to the Irish College
in Rome, where he was to study for the
next four years. He was ordained a priest
on 22 February 1964. Whilst in Rome,
he studied at the Lateran University and
obtained a Licentiate in Theology. He
was in Rome for the first two sessions of
Vatican Council II. As a student, he was
given the responsibility of looking after
the Irish bishops who stayed in the Irish
College.

Dr Clifford's first post after ordination
was as a teacher and Dean of Discipline
in St Brendan's College, Killarney,
where he taught from 1964 to 1972. He
commuted to Cork five days per week
(1965-66) for his HDip in Education. He
was later to lecture on a part-time basis
in UCC in Social Science (1975-81). He
is now a member of the Governing Body
representing north and south Tipperary.

Dr Clifford then studied Social
Administration at the London School of
Economics (1972-74), where he was
conferred with a Master's Degree with
distinction. From London, he returned
to his native Kerry in August 1974 to
become Diocesan Secretary. During that
time he also served as Chaplain at St
Mary of the Angels, Beaufort, a home
for children with learning disabilities.

On 24 December 1985, Dr Clifford was
appointed Coadjutor Archbishop of
Cashel. Most Rev Dr Thomas Morris,
Archbishop of Cashel, ordained him
Bishop on 9 March 1986. He was parish
priest of Tipperary town for two and a
half years. On 12 September 1988 he was
installed as Archbishop of Cashel and
Emly in a ceremony in Thurles Cathedral
presided over by the late Cardinal Tomás
Ó Fiaich.

A keen footballer in his earlier years, he
became the first Kerryman to hold the
office of Patron of the Gaelic Athletic
Association, in 1989. That same year he
was awarded a PhD degree for a thesis
on *Carers of the Elderly and Handicapped*
at the Loughborough University; this
was based on studies he conducted in
Kerry just before he left.

Dr Clifford has served on the Emigrant
Commission of the Bishops' Conference
and he helped to set up the Chaplaincy
Scheme to the young emigrants in the
USA in 1987. He is currently Chairman
of the Irish Bishop's Research and
Development Commission. He is a
Trustee of the *Bóthar* project, which
sends livestock to Uganda and other
countries recovering from the effects of
war and famine.

Cathedral of the Assumption, Thurles

The Cathedral of the Assumption stands
on the site of earlier chapels. The first
church on this site was part of the
Carmelite priory, which dates from the
early fourteenth century.

Some time before 1730 George Mathew,
Catholic proprietor of the Thurles
Estate, built a chapel for the Catholics
of Thurles beside the ruins of the
Carmelite priory. It was known as the
Mathew Chapel. In 1810 Archbishop
Bray consecrated the new 'Big Chapel',
which was more spacious and ornate
than its humble predecessor.

Soon after his appointment as
archbishop in 1857, Dr Patrick Leahy
revealed his plan to replace the Big
Chapel with 'a cathedral worthy of the
archdiocese'. Building commenced in
1865, and the impressive Romanesque
cathedral, with its façade modelled on
that of Pisa, was consecrated by Archbishop Croke on 21 June 1879. The

...hitect was J. J. McCarthy. Barry
...cMullen was the main builder, and
...C. Ashlin was responsible for the
...closing walls, railing and much of the
...ished work.

...e cathedral has many beautiful
...tures, including an impressive rose
...ndow, a free-standing baptistry and a
...ignificent altar. The prize possession of
...e cathedral is its exquisite tabernacle,
...e work of Giacomo dello Porta (1537-
...2), a pupil of Michelangelo. This
...ernacle, which belonged to the Gesú
...suit) Church in Rome, was purchased
...Archbishop Leahy and transported to
...urles.

...e cathedral was extensively renovated
...1 the sanctuary sympathetically
...nodelled on the occasion of its first
...tenary in 1979.

Derrynaflan Chalice

The Derrynaflan Hoard (chalice, paton and wine strainer) was discovered on a Sunday afternoon, 17 February 1980, in the environs of the ancient monastic settlement of Derrynaflan, an island in Littleton Bog, Co Tipperary.

Emly

Archdiocese of
Cashel & Diocese of Emly

HISTORY OF THE DIOCESE

THE UNION of the Archdiocese of Cashel and the Diocese of Emly was formally effected in 1718, sixty-seven years after the last Bishop of Emly, Blessed Terence Albert O'Brien, died for the faith on a Limerick scaffold when Cromwellian forces under Henry Ireton captured the city in late October 1651. Since that date and, indeed, for long centuries before, both dioceses shared a similar historical experience.

SAINTS, SINNERS AND SCHOLARS
Both Cashel and Emly dioceses have their origins in the early Christian period in Ireland. St Ailbe's famous monastic settlement at Emly most likely pre-dated the arrival of St Patrick in Ireland. The origins of the Archdiocese of Cashel are more obscure. As an important political centre, it is likely that Cashel had its own bishop from an early date. While Emly was the leading ecclesiastical centre in Munster for a number of centuries, the growing importance of the Eoghanacht dynasty ensured Cashel's increasing prominence in Church affairs.

The upheaval caused by the Viking advance resulted for a time in the vesting of secular and ecclesiastical authority in the hands of a number of colourful king-bishops in Cashel. Understandably, this uneasy union of crown and crozier did not always enhance the cause of religion. However, not all king-bishops in Cashel followed the example of the ambitious and bellicose Feidhlimid, who perished on a Leinster battlefield in 841. The saintly Cormac Mac Cuilleanáin (901-8) was a rare embodiment of monastic holiness and scholarship allied to wise and peaceful rule.

Emly's famous monastic school and the beautiful Derrynaflan Chalice serve to exemplify the remarkable achievement of the monastic church period in the dioceses of Cashel and Emly.

MEDIEVAL EBB AND FLOW
The arrival of the Gregorian reform movement in twelfth-century Ireland

hastened the replacement of a pre-dominantly monastic Church structure by a regular diocesan system. Cashel's metropolitan status dates from this period. The reform also accelerated the introduction into Ireland of numerous new and renewed orders of monks, canons and friars. Both Cashel and Emly had many houses of these Religious throughout the late medieval period.

The beautifully impressive Cormac's Chapel on the Rock of Cashel represents Irish links with medieval Germany. Holycross Abbey, founded in 1180 and restored as a parish church in the 1970s, ranks among the famous late medieval Irish Cistercian monasteries.

The initial vitality of this medieval era gave way, in time, to stagnation and decline. However, a promising renewal was gathering momentum during the fifteenth century. Sadly, this renewal was interrupted by the arrival of the Protestant Reformation in the next century.

REFORMATION, OPPRESSION, SURVIVAL
The story of the Reformation period in both Cashel and Emly is a mixture of trial and triumph. Political considerations largely dictated the pace and extent to which the new Protestant State religion and Church would be imposed. In the end, the great majority of the people remained loyal to the old faith, though at a considerable price. From the late sixteenth century until the early eighteenth century, intermittent persecution, increasing powerlessness and deprivation were the lot of Irish Catholics.

The prominence of Cashel and Emly laity, bishops, priests and religious among the Irish martyrs of the period is testimony to remarkable fidelity in the face of persecution and oppression. The most famous of these martyrs is Blessed Dermot O'Hurley, Archbishop of Cashel, who was subjected to cruel torture before being martyred in Dublin in 1584. No less inspiring is the example of the victims of massacres in Moor Abbey, Galbally, in 1570 and on the Rock of Cashel in 1647.

The significant Irish clerical and lay Diaspora in Europe during these

centuries is fittingly represented by Cashel priest, Fr Theobald Stapleton, whose famous Catechism for use on the Irish mission was composed in Brussels in 1639.

REBUILDING THE EDIFICE
As the Penal Laws were relaxed from the middle of the eighteenth century, Thurles became the new permanent place of residence for the archbishops of Cashel and Emly. At the same time we glimpse in the pages of the Visitation Book of Archbishop James Butler I (1757-74) the gradual emergence of a newly vibrant, though impoverished, Church of the People. This renewed Catholicism gathered momentum from the late eighteenth century and culminated in a remarkable array of Catholic institutions ministering to the spiritual and temporal needs of the people. In Cashel and Emly the faith and generosity of a newly emancipated people built, supported and staffed churches, schools, colleges and other charitable institutions over the past two hundred years. This achievement is all the more remarkable when it is remembered that it occurred in the midst of widespread poverty and massive emigration, with limited State assistance at best.

The era of renewal and consolidation, which now appears to be changing, is also characterised by a remarkable commitment of personnel and resources to the needs of the wider Church. In common with the entire Irish Church, the Archdiocese of Cashel and Emly can be proud of its contribution to the development of Catholicism throughout the English-speaking world, especially through the work of St Patrick's College, Thurles. No less impressive is the work of the many Cashel and Emly missionaries who served in Africa, Asia and, more recently South America. The lives and ministry of Bishop Shanahan in Southern Nigeria and Bishop Thomas Quinlan in China and Korea are fitting testimony to the generosity and courage of the many other missionaries from Cashel and Emly, and the entire Irish Church, during the past century and a half.

HOPEFUL FUTURE

The historian's craft is to record and assess the past, not to predict the future. Nevertheless, the generous fidelity of Mobal Ailbe, the faithful of Cashel and Emly, over so many centuries inspires confidence that present and future challenges to faith and Church can be successfully negotiated. How the rich heritage of faith that we have inherited is offered to future generations will be part of the history of Cashel and Emly in the new millennium.

PLACE OF PILGRIMAGE

Holy Cross Abbey

Holy Cross Abbey is one of the most important ecclesiastical centres in the archdiocese.

There were monks in Uachtar-amhan (the ancient Celtic name for Holy Cross) before the Cistercians came from Monasterneagh, Co Limerick.

1180: Donal Mór O'Briain endowed the abbey 'in honour of the Almighty God, the Blessed Virgin Mary and St Benedict and the Holy Cross'.

1400-50: Extensive reconstruction of the church and abbey.
1563: Abbey and possessions granted to Thomas Butler, Earl of Ormond, by Queen Elizabeth I. Some monks remained on and pilgrimages continued.
1583: Dermot O'Hurley, Archbishop of Cashel and martyr for the faith, visited the abbey as a pilgrim.
1600: January: O'Neill of Ulster at abbey. November: Hugh O'Donnell at abbey.
1640: Brother John (Malachy Harty) compiled chronicle of the abbey ('Triupmhalia Chronologica' or Triumphant History of Holy Cross).
1740: Last Cistercian monk of Holy Cross died.
1880: Abbey church vested in the State as a National Monument.
1969: Act of Oireachtas passed enabling the Abbey church to be restored and used as the parish church.
1970: Archaeological excavation of church site.
1971: Restoration of church commenced.
1975: Restoration completed and church brought into use again as the parish church.

Holy Cross Abbey, located on the bank of the River Suir, four miles south-west of Thurles, has seen eight centuries of Irish history. It was founded for the Cistercians about 1180 by Donal Mór Ua'Briain (O'Brien), King of Limerick.

The abbey took its name from a notable relic of the True Cross enshrined within it at the time of its foundation, which made it a foremost place of pilgrimage up to the seventeenth century.

After being roofless and out of use for well over two hundred years, Holy Cross has come into prominence again. The Abbey church, one of the finest examples of Gothic architecture in Ireland's heritage, has been painstakingly restored to serve as a parish church, rededicated to the Holy Cross.

In the early 1960s it was decided to fully restore the abbey. This idea was the brainchild of the Most Rev Dr Thomas Morris, Archbishop of Cashel and Emly. The restoration was completed in 1975. Since then it has continued to serve the archdiocese and the parish church of Holy Cross. It is one of the few roofless and abandoned medieval churches in the country to be restored for use.

Archdiocese of Tuam

Most Rev Michael Neary DD

Michael Neary was born in Castlebar on 15 April 1946. Having received his early education at St Patrick's National School, Castlebar and St Jarlath's College, Tuam, he studied for the priesthood at St Patrick's College, Maynooth, and was ordained in 1971. After a year on the staff of St Jarlath's College he returned to Maynooth for postgraduate studies in theology, where he was awarded the Doctorate in Divinity in 1975. He served as curate in Belclare for one year before being appointed to the staff of Presentation College, Headford, Co Galway.

From 1978 to 1981 he did postgraduate studies at the Pontifical Biblical Institute in Rome, for which he was awarded the Licentiate in Sacred Scripture. During that time he was Spiritual Director at the Irish College. On his return he joined the staff of Holy Rosary College, Mountbellew, and served as curate in Moylough. In 1982 he was appointed Lecturer in Sacred Scripture at Maynooth and became Professor of New Testament in 1991.

He is a member of the theology department of the Irish Inter-Church Meeting which deals with ecumenical matters. He is a former member of the editorial board of the *Irish Theological Quarterly*. In 1990 he published 'Our Hide and Seek God', based on retreats for priests, which he had given throughout the country.

He was consecrated Titular Bishop of Quaestoriana and Auxiliary to the Archbishop of Tuam at the Basilica of Our Lady, Queen of Ireland, Knock on 13 September 1992. Following on the retirement of Archbishop Cassidy, Bishop Neary was appointed Archbishop of Tuam and installed on 5 March 1995. He is Chairman of the Episcopal Commission for Emigrants and sits on the Episcopal Commission for Theology.

The O'Queely Plate

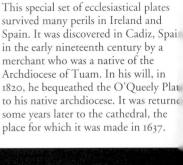

The picture contains some of what is known in Tuam as the O'Queely Plate. Archbishop Malachy O'Queely (1630-45) commissioned this unique set for Tuam cathedral in 1637. There are eleven pieces in all – some silver gilt, some silver ungilt. The chalice weighs over three pounds. The archbishop's Coat of Arms and the date are engraved on some of the pieces and erased from others.

This special set of ecclesiastical plates survived many perils in Ireland and Spain. It was discovered in Cadiz, Spain in the early nineteenth century by a merchant who was a native of the Archdiocese of Tuam. In his will, in 1820, he bequeathed the O'Queely Plate to his native archdiocese. It was returned some years later to the cathedral, the place for which it was made in 1637.

Includes half of County Mayo, half of County Galway and part of County Roscommon

Cathedral of the Assumption, Tuam

The Cathedral of the Assumption is the metropolitan cathedral of the Western Province.

Archbishop Oliver Kelly (1815-34) laid the foundation stone on 30 April 1827 – before Catholic Emancipation. The cathedral was dedicated on 18 August 1836 by Archbishop John MacHale (1834-81). It cost £14,204.

The cathedral is English-decorated Gothic in style, is cruciform in shape and has a three-stage West Tower. It was designed by architect Dominick Madden. Nineteen windows light the cathedral. It has seating capacity for 1,100 people.

Among the cathedral's notable features are its superbly cut Galway and Mayo limestone, its plaster-vaulted ceiling with heads and bosses, and its cantilevered oak organ loft. Its huge Oriel window has eighty-two compartments, is forty-two feet high and eighteen feet wide; it is the work of Michael O'Connor and was made in Dublin in 1832. Four large windows from the Harry Clarke studio also grace the cathedral. It has a very fine Compton organ with 1200 pipes, a unique set of early nineteenth-century Stations of the Cross, recently restored, and a seventeenth-century painting of the Assumption by Carlo Maratta.

The sanctuary, as shown above, was completely redesigned in 1991 under the direction of the late Ray Carroll. The altar is Wicklow granite, and all the timberwork is by local craftsman Tom Dowd.

Archdiocese of Tuam

HISTORY OF THE DIOCESE

TUAM DIOCESE, stretching from Achill Island to Moore parish on the Shannon, a distance of 120 miles, is the largest in the country. Geographically split north/south by the two lakes, Loughs Mask and Corrib, Tuam has pastoral charge of the largest Gaeltacht area in the country and of six of Ireland's island parishes. It also contains the major pilgrimage centres of Knock Shrine and Croagh Patrick. Established by the twelfth-century synods of Rathbreasail and Kells, it subsequently absorbed two other medieval dioceses: Annaghdown and Mayo.

Although not listed in Rathbreasail or Kells, Annaghdown diocese survived nonetheless for many centuries through monastic outreach from Annaghdown Abbey. Several 'bishops of Annaghdown', from 1189 to 1485, were systematically elected by its 'Cathedral Chapter' and, despite many counter-claims from Tuam, some were approved by Rome. In 1485, when the Wardenship of Galway was created, Annaghdown was formally united with Tuam by Papal decree, and some of its parishes, Claregalway, Moycullen and Shrule, were formally attached to the new wardenship.

The Diocese of Mayo, though recognised officially in the Synod of Kells, was suppressed in the thirteenth century. Bishops were appointed, however, as late as the sixteenth century. One of its bishops, Patrick O'Hely, who died in 1589, is numbered among the Irish martyr saints. The diocese was formally joined to Tuam by Papal decree in 1631.

The absence of continuity in territory makes Tuam's diocesan boundary unique. Moore parish and the Kilmeen portion of Leitrim parish, both situated within Clonfert diocese, have been part of Tuam since medieval times. Shrule parish, now part of Galway diocese, is nestled in the Tuam geographical area on the east of Lough Corrib. Originally, it belonged to the medieval Diocese of Cong. But in south Connemara, 'extra-territorial' enclaves alternate between Tuam and Galway in a patchwork pattern. This situation may be explained by a number of factors: Galway's late emergence as a diocese in 1831; the unusual topography of islands, inlets and lakes; and the late population settlements in Connemara. Also, there was the influence of Annaghdown diocese, stretching across Lough Corrib. To rectify the situation, an exchange took place with Galway of one of those parishes, Killannin, for parts of Carraroe in 1890, but this created enormous disturbance and formed only a partial solution.

Tuam has its own quota of acclaimed saints: Jarlath of Tuam, Feichín of Cong, Macdara of Carna, Colman of Inisboffin, Fursey of Headford, Enda of Aran, Benin of Kilbannon and Cuana of Kilcoona, amongst others.

CHURCHES
Even after the Synod of Kells, a multiplicity of abbeys had pastoral care for the people in their surroundings. With the despoliation of the monasteries and the scarcity of priests during penal days, old churches were abandoned. Where they were replaced, it was with miserable thatched shelters. House 'stations' were a necessary substitute for normal public worship. In 1825, Archbishop Kelly testified before a House of Commons Committee of Enquiry that out of 107 places of worship in the diocese, only eighteen had slated roofs. The others, he said, were thatched and wretched, insufficient to contain the congregations, and in many instances the public prayers were celebrated in the open air. The chapels were also used as Sunday schools, and a great many were used on weekdays as the local school.

As persecution abated, and as priests became more plentiful, a new confidence grew and the small thatched buildings were superseded by more solid, ample structures. Only two of the existing churches in the diocese precede 1800 – the abbeys of Ballyhaunis and Ballintubber. But from 1820 onwards, a phenomenal rate of construction began. Twenty of the 135 existing churches were constructed in the Famine years, 1840-1850. The pattern of church replacement or reconstruction continued to modern times. Modern church architecture is rare in Tuam diocese, as most churches pre-date the modern era. The four special chapels constructed at Knock Shrine, including the Basilica, since 1972 are, however, of special importance.

EDUCATION
In the nineteenth century, Tuam had a late start in primary education as Archbishop Mc Hale had a great antipathy to the National School Education Acts. In nine rural areas where proselytism was a problem, he had the Third Order of St Francis provide schools, but, on the whole, primary education was patchy. There was still much reliance on payschools and the efforts of local people, or on landlords, benign or otherwise. Religious-run schools were confined largely to the towns. In the twentieth century, however, Tuam diocese, under Archbishop Walsh, was to the fore in the provision of secondary schools, especially in the twenty-year period before 1967, when the State made building grants and 'free' post-primary education available. Two extra diocesan colleges were established as well as nine co-educational schools in small towns throughout the diocese, the latter managed by religious, usually in conjunction with priests of the diocese. As a result, a whole generation of pupils had the advantage of secondary education and many thereby escaped the emigrant ship.

POPULATION CHANGES
In 1800 there were no more than one hundred priests in the diocese. The number grew steadily to 170 about 1968 despite the fact that the population had dropped to less than 30% of what it had been before the Famine. The number has now dropped to approximately 150, and of these, more than twenty are on loan from missionary orders. The devotion of the people remained strong in all these years. In 1986, the figure attending Mass in the archdiocese was approximately 75% of the whole Catholic population,

r 89% of those obliged to attend Mass. This has decreased by approximately o% in recent years. A major survey of he diocese carried out in 1996 found hat the pattern of population decline is till continuing; nowadays, however, that ecline continues through out-migration o the eastern part of Ireland, but with he same deleterious effects on the west.

PLACE OF PILGRIMAGE

KNOCK SHRINE
Knock Shrine is now the largest pilgrimge centre in Ireland, attracting pilgrims rom every part of Ireland, from Europe, nd indeed all five continents.

The origin of the devotion is the laimed apparition of Our Blessed Lady, vith St Joseph and St John, on 21 August 1879. The event was subjected to he most exhaustive Church enquiries nd, subsequently, in 1936, before the ast of the witnesses to the apparition ied, both tribunals found the evidence f the witnesses 'upright and rustworthy'. The number of xtraordinary cures and favours ssociated with Knock from the earliest ears caused the pilgimage to grow. Pope John Paul II visited the shrine on o September 1979.

Almost one million pilgrims visit the hrine annually. Organised groups come rom May to October and private ilgrimages take place on almost every ay of the year. Pilgrims are cared for by thousand voluntary helpers, the Knock

Shrine Stewards and Handmaids. The Annual Novena, from 14 to 22 August, attracts up to 100,000 people. The shrine grounds and five chapels at Knock make it a place of great beauty, conducive to prayerfulness and peace.

The pilgrimage itself includes a visit to the Blessed Sacrament in any one of the five chapels on the grounds; the Stations of the Cross; the fifteen mysteries of the Rosary, five of which are recited while the pilgrim walks around the Church. The celebration of Mass is usually a central part of the pilgrimage, as is the celebration of the Sacrament of Reconciliation.

CROAGH PATRICK
Documentary evidence associating Croagh Patrick, or 'The Reek', as it is affectionately known, with St Patrick's forty days of fasting there, goes back at least to the seventh-century account of Bishop Tirechán. The traditional pilgrimage is mentioned in several documents from 1300 and it is certain that the pilgrimage extends back at least one thousand years.

Formerly a pre-Christian shrine, called Sliabh Aigli, it has been hallowed by St Patrick and by Christian footsteps and prayers through the centuries. The traditional date of the pilgrimage is the last Sunday of July – or, for the local people, the Friday beforehand, called 'Garland Friday'. Nowadays, the pilgrimage takes place from early morning, but until the 1970s pilgrims

climbed the mountain in the darkness and were on the summit for the first of the morning Masses at daybreak. Private pilgrimages also take place on most days of the summer.

The traditional 'station', as distinct from the climb, begins at the eastern base of the cone at Leacht Benain, where the pilgrim walks seven rounds of the *leacht* and then climbs to the top by way of the steep passage known locally as 'the ladder'. One walks fifteen times around Teampall Phádraig on top, seven times around each of the three mounds of Roilig Mhuire and seven times around the area of Garraí Mhór on the western slope. A corresponding number of Paters and Aves and the Gloria and the Creed are said at each one of these.

The pilgrimage is not suitable for people in poor health.

BALLINTUBBER ABBEY
Ballintubber Abbey, Co Mayo, founded in 1216, is unique in that it is the oldest medieval Catholic parish church in Ireland still in use.

The abbey itself has been restored in several stages since 1890, and in recent years, Tóchar Phádraig, the twenty-two-mile walking pilgrimage along the traditional pilgrim route used by St Patrick from Ballintubber to Croagh Patrick, has been revived. The three-day pilgrimage to Ballintubber now also includes one full day of solitude and reflection on nearby 'Church Island', in Lough Carra, where an eighth-century hermit's church has been restored.

LOCAL PILGRIMAGES IN THE ARCHDIOCESE OF TUAM
15 August and May-October: Lady's Well, Athenry, since AD 1249.
9 June: Tobar Choilmchille, Baile na hAbhann, Connemara.
15 July: Oileán Mhic Dara, Carna, Connemara.
First Sunday of August: Patrician Shrine at Máméan, Recess, Connemara.
Garland Friday, July: Croagh Patrick – pilgrimage for local people.
20 August: Pilgrimage to St Bernard's Well, Abbeyknockmoy, Co Galway.
Through the year: St Patrick's Well, Kilgeever, Louisburgh.
May-October: Tóchar Phádraig – Ballintubber Abbey to Croagh Patrick.
May-October: Church Island, Lough Carra, part of Ballintubber pilgrimage.

Diocese of
Achonry

Most Rev Thomas Flynn DD

Son of Robert and Margaret Flynn (née Carty) from Aughalustia in the cathedral parish of Ballaghaderreen (Castlemore and Kilcolman), Thomas Flynn was born on 8 July 1931. He attended the local primary school in Aughalustia and later the De La Salle Brothers' school in Ballaghaderreen. From there, he went to St Nathy's Diocesan College in Ballaghaderreen as a dayboy, and then to St Patrick's College, Maynooth in 1949, where he studied Philosophy and Theology.

After ordination, he served as Chaplain to the St John of God Sisters in Ballinamore, Co Mayo and later to the Marist Sisters in Tubbercurry, Co Sligo, combining chaplaincy work with being Religious Adviser to schools. In 1964 he joined the teaching staff at St Nathy's College as teacher of Greek, Latin, Irish and English. He was appointed President and Headmaster of the College in 1973. Four years later, in February 1977, he was ordained Bishop of Achonry.

As bishop, he has served on the Bishops' Commission for Communications, where for some years he acted as Spokesman for the Bishops' Conference. In Education, he headed the Bishops' Commission in contributing to the New Education Act of 1998, and he is still Chairman of that Commission. He played a smaller role in the Laity and Social Welfare Commissions. For many years he was Visitor to the Irish College in Rome and at present he is a Visitor to Maynooth College. As bishop, he has promoted Adult Religious Education through the building of a Pastoral Centre in Charlestown, and Adult Religious Formation through many programmes, especially through the process called 'Renew'. There are now two diocesan centres and a number of parish centres for religious education. There is a Family Therapy Centre run by the Sisters of Mercy in Ballaghaderreen for families and individuals in need of counselling and help. In Foxford, the Sisters of Mercy, too, have with diocesan

help turned a former convent into an addiction-treatment centre – Hope House – a symbol of hope and light for those whose lives have been darkened and damaged by alcohol, drugs and gambling.

Cathedral of the Annunciation and St Nathy, Ballaghaderreen

The building of the cathedral was begun in 1855 by Bishop Durcan. The architects were Messrs Hadfield & Goldie of Sheffield, while the Clerk of Works was Mr Charles Barker. It was completed in 1860.

The style is simple Gothic, known as Early English, of the Gothic Revival. The original intention was to have the roof fan-vaulted in wood and plaster, but it was abandoned owing to cost, and was finished in open timbers. The plan for a spire also had to be abandoned. This, however, was built in 1905 by Bishop Lyster, and a carillon of bells was installed.

The organ was built with continental pipes by Chestnutt of Waterford in 1925. The sanctuary was reconstructed to conform to the liturgical reforms of Vatican II in 1972. The baptistry in the left-hand Side Chapel was donated by Lydia Viscountess Dillon in memory of Charles Henry Viscount Dillon who died on 18 November 1865. The Apostles' Creed is carved on the baptistry lid.

There are commemorative plaques to former bishops of Achonry in the left-hand Side Chapel: Bishops McNicholas Durcan, Lyster and Morrisroe.

The window in the Lady Chapel has the inscription: 'This window to the Glory of God and Honour of the Blessed Virgin Mary was erected by united subscription of the Bishop, Clergy and 19 inhabitants of the Parish and neighbourhood to commemorate their respect and esteem for Charles Strickland and his wife Maria of Loughglynn and their zealous assistance in the erection of the Cathedral Church in 1860'. Charles Strickland was agent for Lord Dillon and was associated with the building of the neighbouring town of Charlestown and its church.

Achonry

Stained-glass windows in the Cathedral of the Annunciation and St Nathy

These two windows in the cathedral depict St John and St Anna. They were designed and painted by Beatrice Elvery (1883-1968), one of Ireland's better-known stained-glass artists. The Túr Gloinne style of work is evident in this pair of windows. (She joined 'An Túr Gloinne' in 1904.)

Diocese of
Achonry

HISTORY OF THE DIOCESE

ST NATHY, a native of Lugne territory, now commensurate with the barony of Leyny in Co Sligo, was appointed over the church of Achonry by St Finian of Clonard just before the latter's death in 552. From the sixth to the twelfth century there is no record of a bishop presiding over Achonry. It was not among the five dioceses assigned to the western province by the Synod of Rathbreasail in 1111, nor does it seem to have been comprised in any of the five, Tuam, Clonfert, Cong, Killala and Ardcairne. Tradition alone claims Achonry to have been an ancient bishopric. It was formally erected by the Synod of Kells in 1152 and had a continuous succession of bishops until the death of Eugene O'Hart OP in 1603. O'Hart, one of three Irish bishops who attended the Council of Trent, was a prominent counter-Reformation bishop in the Irish Church in the sixteenth century. He lived to be a hundred and was recorded by government officials to be administering Confirmation in the vicinity of Mallow, Co Cork, when he was well into his nineties.

From 1603 to 1707 there was no bishop in Achonry and the diocese was administered by apostolic vicars. For most of the eighteenth century there was no resident bishop in the diocese. Yet, during this period, though persecuted and impoverished, a vibrant Church flourished, with its own homespun and all-pervasive spirituality and rituals. Without churches or institutional infrastructure, religion became people-centred. All the important ceremonies took place in the homes – Masses, christenings, confessions, weddings and wakes. It was a celebratory Church, enjoying its wakes no less than its weddings. In the absence of churches, holy wells became popular centres of devotion. Pilgrimages were made to them, particularly during 'patterns', patrons' feastdays. Wells dedicated to St Attracta, patron of Achonry, were scattered throughout the diocese and

drew crowds of pilgrims on her feastday, 11 August. Though no very reliable records of her life remain, she is reputed to have been a contemporary of St Patrick, to whom she made her profession in Coolavin near Lough Gara. St Patrick founded a nunnery there and appointed Attracta its first abbess. The church there, Killaraght, is named after her. (See Liam Swords, *A Hidden Church: The Diocese of Achonry 1689-1818*.)

With Catholic education proscribed by law, hedge-schools abounded, and young priests, ordained at home, went to one of the many Irish continental colleges for their theological training. Most returned to the Irish mission. Among those who did not was Andrew Donlevy who was appointed superior of the student community of the Irish College, Paris. There, in 1742, he published his famous Irish-English *Catechism*. Many of the Catholic aristocracy also sought careers in Europe. Most famous of these was the Dillon family, Viscounts of Costello-Gallen, the most extensive landlord in the diocese, who remained Catholic until almost the end of the eighteenth century. In France they established the famous Dillon Regiment. One of the last of them, Arthur, was guillotined during the French Revolution. Another Achonry family, the Taaffes of Ballymote, won distinction in the Austrian service. Further afield, Admiral Browne from Foxford became the founder of the Argentinian navy.

Others earned immortality at home, notably the poets Seán Ó Gadhra and Anthony Raftery (1779-1835). The famous harpist, Turlough O'Carolan (1670-1738), though not a native of the diocese, was a frequent visitor. The diocese became the heart of what was later called 'O'Carolan country' and his compositions read like a Who's Who of Achonry. Among his compositions was *Seán Ó Hairt,* who was bishop of the diocese from 1735 to 1739.

With the Catholic relief measures late in the eighteenth century, the Church emerged from the underground, building barn chapels, which later in the

nineteenth century were replaced by more imposing churches, most of them still in use. These were generally located in the new emerging towns, and a new institutionalised, town-based Church replaced its rural, home-centred predecessor. The nineteenth century was dominated by the awful calamity of the Great Famine, in which Achonry, one of the poorest and over-populated districts of the country, suffered more than most (See Liam Swords, *In Their Own Words, the Famine in North Connacht, 1845-49*.) The cottier class, the backbone of the earlier Church, was decimated by death and emigration. A new Catholic middle class emerged, consisting of strong farmers and shopkeepers, of whom the parish priest became the social and political as well as spiritual leader. The clergy played a prominent role in the Repeal Movement and later in the Land League and Home Rule Movement. Achonry provided some of the prominent figures on the national stage. John Blake Dillon, who was born in Ballaghaderreen, was a Young Irelander who co-founded *The Nation* with Thomas Davis and Charles Gavan Duffy. His son John, who later inherited the family business in Ballaghaderreen, was a leading figure in the Plan of Campaign and leader of the Home Rule Party after the Parnellite split. He was defeated in East Mayo by de Valera in the 1918 election. His son, James, later became leader of Fine Gael. Perhaps the most famous native of Achonry was Michael Davitt who was born in Straide in 1846. His family later emigrated to England, where Davitt, was imprisoned as a young man for his Fenian activities. On his release he returned to Ireland, where he founded the Land League. The meeting at Gurteen, Co Sligo and the subsequent arrest and trial of the leaders launched the League into national and international prominence. The under-secretary, Sir Anthony McDonnell, was also an Achonry man who achieved distinction in the colonial service in India before returning to Ireland. He ended his political career as the Baron of Swinford in the House of Lords.

Fr Denis O'Hara, parish priest of Kiltimagh, was one of the leading clergymen of his day. One of the early activists in the Land League, he later became a member of the Congested Districts Board, a position he retained until his death in 1922.

PLACE OF PILGRIMAGE

Massrock, Masshill, Parish of Cloonacool

The statue of St Patrick erected on the rock, was put there in 1979 to replace the statue that had been erected in 1929 to commemorate the first centenary of Catholic Emancipation. It stands on what is traditionally known as the Massrock.

Recently fourteen crosses were erected on the hill leading to the rock and these are numbered as Stations of the Cross. Each year, on Good Friday evening, the wood of the cross is carried to the Massrock and erected there with a white cloth draped around it. The religious service is well attended and is attempted in all weathers. Many now come to see the rock and are prompted to pray by the fourteen stations.

Mass is also celebrated there on 21 June (the summer solstice) in honour of Christ who is the light of the world. This is also well attended and takes place in all weathers.

Diocese of
Ardagh and Clonmacnois

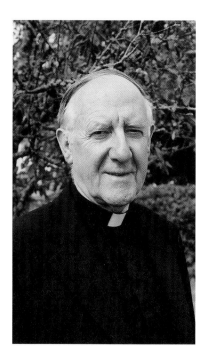

Most Rev Colm O'Reilly DD

Bishop Colm O'Reilly was born on 11 January 1935 to John and Alicia O'Reilly of the parish of Colmcille in the Diocese of Ardagh and Clonmacnois. His eldest brother, Peter, who died in 1988, was Superior General of St Patrick's Missionary Society for sixteen years. Another brother, Brendan, is a member of the Divine Word Missionaries and is currently ministering in Kenya.

Colm O'Reilly attended primary school in his native parish and subsequently went to St Mel's College in Longford. He was ordained a priest in Maynooth on 19 June 1960.

Following his ordination, he spent his entire life as a priest in parishes in the Diocese of Ardagh and Clonmacnois. He ministered for nine years in Granard, and until the time of his appointment as Bishop of Ardagh and Clonmacnois on 10 April 1983, he was curate and later administrator at St Mel's Cathedral.

As bishop, he has served the Episcopal Conference as President of Accord and of the Laity Commission, of which he is still President. He is also currently President of Cura and a member of the National Mission Council and the Pastoral Commission.

St Mel's Cathedral, Longford

On 19 May 1840, Bishop William O'Higgins laid the foundation stone of a new cathedral for the Diocese of Ardagh and Clonmacnois. The foundation stone was taken from the original Cathedral of St Mel at Ardagh. The preacher at that ceremony was the Archbishop of Tuam, Archbishop John MacHale. Four other bishops, one hundred and twenty priests and an estimated forty thousand people were present.

The architect of the cathedral was Mr John Benjamin Keane. The magnificent portico was not included in the original design. This was the work of another architect, Mr George Ashlin, and was not erected until 1883. Without any doubt Bishop O'Higgins influenced the original design, which reflected some of his own life experience, having been educated in Paris, Rome and having lived for a time in Vienna. The cathedral owes something in its design to the Madeleine in Paris, and the Pantheon and the Basilica of St John Lateran in Rome. Certainly something of the Lateran is to be seen in the attempt that was made to incorporate the bishop's house at the rear of the sanctuary.

Raising the money necessary to build the cathedral was an enormous challenge in poverty-stricken Ireland in the 1840s. Bishop O'Higgins travelled the length and breadth of the diocese and his appeals for help went well beyond the diocesan boundaries. He received great help, especially from the Dioceses of Elphin, Tuam and Meath, and contributions came from as far away as Belfast. A priest of the diocese toured North America and Canada to raise funds there.

By 1846 the walls, pillars and entire masonry were completed and the roof was the next stage in the building programme. Then the potato blight came and the Great Hunger. Work had to be suspended. Bishop O'Higgins would never see the great cathedral completed. He died in 1853. Bishop John Kilduff, successor of Bishop O'Higgins, resumed work on the cathedral. It was opened for worship in September 1856. Though the work was not complete, it was a time of great rejoicing. Present on that special day were Archbishop Dixon of Armagh and Archbishop Cullen of Dublin, and fourteen other bishops.

It was Bishop Bartholomew Woodlock who commissioned the erection of the impressive portico, with its huge Ionic columns. He was still bishop of the diocese in 1893 when the cathedral was consecrated on 19 May.

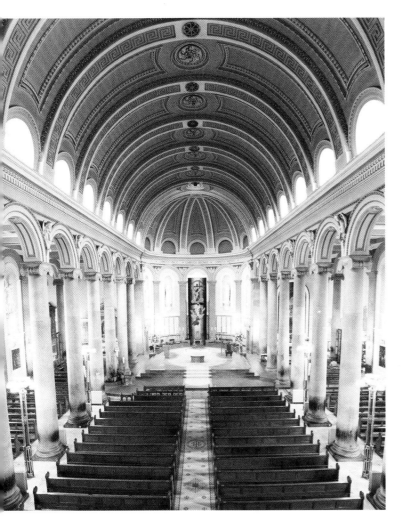

Since 1893 much additional work has been done. Bishop Hoare, successor of Bishop Woodlock, added a pipe organ and bell chimes. Later still, two beautiful stained-glass windows, the work of the Harry Clarke Studios in Dublin, were installed in the transepts. In the 1970s a major restyling of the sanctuary was undertaken.

St Manchan's Shrine

Though damaged, St Manchan's Shrine is one of the masterpieces of Irish Christian art. A house-shaped box of yew-wood has been cased in bronze, and the whole elaborately gilded and enamelled. Most of the ornamental work is of mixed Viking and Irish styles, which date the main body of the shrine to around 1125 – there are close parallels with the Cross of Cong. What are controversial are the human figures, which reflect continental influence. Were they part of the original composition, a daring marrying of the Hiberno-Norse and the Romanesque, or were they added a generation later to update a masterpiece that was beginning to look old-fashioned? What has confused the issue is the fact that a twelfth-century workshop in Ireland was producing these figures in quantity – an unhappy modern addition is one found at Clonmacnois, and others have been found in counties Roscommon and Derry. One of the original figures from the shrine, that holding an axe, has been identified in a recent paper as depicting St Olaf of Norway. If this is right, it is the earliest known representation of that saint, who died in 1027, was being invoked by Irish Vikings in 1052, and relics of whom were in Christ Church, Dublin, before 1074.

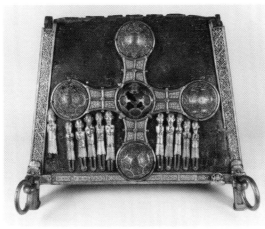

Diocese of
Ardagh & Clonmacnois

HISTORY OF THE DIOCESE

THE DIOCESE of Ardagh, as distinct from that of Clonmacnois, with which it is now united, takes its name from the very picturesque village of Ardagh in Co Longford. That St Patrick came to Ardagh and founded a church there is attested by two of our earliest sources of information on his life and labours, the Memoir of Tirechán in the *Book of Armagh* and the Tripartite *Life*. It is the privilege of the Diocese of Ardagh to have as its patron and first bishop one of St Patrick's immediate entourage, his friend, and, according to some, his nephew, St Mel. Thus the history of Ardagh goes back to the dawn of Christianity in Ireland, and its episcopal succession to one of the primitive Fathers of the Irish Church.

Though the original organisation of the Irish Church was episcopal and diocesan, it soon tended to become monastic. The oldest of the monastic institutions in the Ardagh part of this diocese may well have been at Ardagh itself. Records of the deaths of some of the bishops of Ardagh are unclear as to whether they were bishops or abbots. The Diocese of Ardagh is dotted with names and, sometimes, the remains of primitive monastic foundations. Among places with a unique claim to fame is Clonbroney. Clonbroney is associated with the earliest recorded 'consecration of virgins' in our history. There St Patrick is said to have given the veil of holy religion to two Emers, sisters of Guasacht and children of Patrick's old slave-master, Milchu. The most famous name in the Annals of Clonbroney is the eighth-century abbess, St Samhthann. She was of royal stock from Ulster and was re-nowned for her virtuous life and the many miracles that were attributed to her.

The most celebrated monastery for many centuries in the Ardagh part of our diocese was that of Inis Clothrann in Lough Ree. The island is supposed to have got its name from Clothra, sister of Maedhbh, the famous Queen of Connaught. Sometimes the island is referred to as Inis Dhiarmada, from the saint who founded its famous monastery. Diarmuid is said to have been the friend and spiritual director of St Ciaran of Clonmacnois.

Another famous monastery in the Diocese of Ardagh was that of Fenagh. Fenagh is now a village in Co Leitrim. A monastery was founded there by St Caillin, who was a contemporary of Ciaran of Clonmacnois. He is associated in the legends with the preservation of the Táin Bó Cuailnge. The recording of the story in *Leabhar na n-Uidhre* links his name with the name of St Ciaran.

Ardagh was erected as a diocese by the Synod of Kells (1152) and was made a suffragan of Armagh. In the thirteenth century a dispute arose as to whether it was subject to Tuam or Armagh. Gregory IX ordered an investigation in 1235 and it was resolved in favour of Armagh.

Of the fifty-nine listed bishops of Ardagh, two were Franciscans, two Augustinians, one a Cistercian and one a Vincentian. For long periods in the seventeenth century and early eighteenth century the diocese was ruled by vicars-apostolic. The diocese featured in the ministry of St Oliver Plunkett, whose relative, Dr Patrick Plunkett, a Cistercian, was bishop of the diocese from 1647 to 1669. Bishop Plunkett was absent from the diocese for almost all of that period and St Oliver Plunkett makes reference to the sad condition into which the Diocese of Ardagh had fallen due to the ravages of persecution. Evidence of the involvement of St Oliver in the diocese is to be seen in the register of priests from 1704, several of whom were ordained by him.

The episcopate of Dr Augustine Cheevers (1751-56) was marked by a significant development. It was during his time as bishop that Clonmacnois was joined to Ardagh permanently. It appears that Bishop Cheevers was administering the Diocese of Clonmacnois on behalf of the bishop of Meath, to which Clonmacnois had been attached at the time when he became bishop. He applied to the Holy See to have Clonmacnois united to Ardagh, saying the poverty of the Diocese of Ardagh was such that he needed additional territory. When he was translated to Meath in 1756 he sought to have this request reversed, but by then the Holy See had acceded to his earlier request and refused to change its mind.

One of the most noteworthy bishops of the Diocese of Ardagh was William O'Higgins, bishop from 1829 to 1853. He was a scholar, a capable and courageous administrator and a man with no small influence on public affairs, civil as well as ecclesiastical. He is best remembered in the diocese for founding St Mel's Cathedral in 1840. Bishop O'Higgins held a Diocesan Synod in 1834, which was attended by forty-one parish priests and forty curates. Five priests were absent because of illness and five more were unable to be present because they had to be on duty. The total number accounts for a presbyterate of ninety-one men.

The Diocese of Clonmacnois has a very different history from that of Ardagh. It was a monastic institution until the Synod of Kells in 1152. This synod followed a series of National Councils of the Irish Church which had sought to establish a proper balance between episcopal and monastic jurisdiction.

Among the most famous Franciscan bishops of Clonmacnois was Anthony MacGeoghagan, a friend and supporter of the Nuncio, Rinuccini. He was named Bishop of Clonmacnois in 1647 and eventually was translated from Clonmacnois to the Diocese of Meath.

Though Clonmacnois is the smaller part of the united dioceses, having just six parishes out of a total of forty-one, its name is the one that is the better known. Its monastic ruins speak eloquently of its great past and can still inspire people.

The missionary spirit that characterised monastic Clonmacnois has a rebirth in the Diocese of Ardagh and Clonmacnois in modern times. In 1932 a priest of the diocese, Monsignor Patrick Whitney, with his cousin, Father Frank Whitney, founded St Patrick's Missionary Society. Close links between the Society and the diocese have kept that spirit alive.

PLACE OF PILGRIMAGE

Clonmacnois

The name Clonmacnois is usually translated into English as: 'the Meadow-land of the sons of Noss'. The origins of the name are vague. It may have begun to be used only after St Ciaran founded his monastery there in 545. Given the fact that Clonmacnois is inseparably associated with St Ciaran, it might be more appropriately named Cluain-Ciarain. His burial place in Clonmacnois has been a place of pilgrimage for over fifteen hundred years of unbroken tradition. The commemoration of his feast on Pattern Day still draws enormous crowds.

Ciaran's ancestry and life history draw all the provinces of Ireland together. His father, Beoit, was a cartwright and chariot-builder from the Kingdom of Dal n-Araide in north-east Ulster. His mother was Darerca, whose ancestors came from Ciarraighe of Irluachra, i.e. in south-east Kerry. Ciaran is thought to have been born at Rathcroghan, though Fuerty is given by many as his birthplace. Thus a Connaught man of Ulster and Munster parents was to spend his active life mainly in Leinster and found his famous monastery there.

Ciaran was trained at the famous school of St Finian at Clonard and is thought to have been ordained a priest during his stay with St Enda on Aran. He is said to have visited St Senan on Scattery Island at the mouth of the Shannon. His own first foundation was on Inis Aingin, now known as Hare Island, on the lower section of Lough Ree, just north of Athlone.

Ciaran chose a magnificent setting for his great monastic foundation. Those who come by boat, preferably down current, get a fabulous view of the monastic ruins from the water. If one assumes that Ciaran and his companions came by that route, pilgrims can still see how well he chose the spot for his monastery.

What the visitor to Clonmacnois sees today is what has lain in ruins since its final destruction in 1552, a testament to the accuracy of the description of the Four Masters: 'Clonmacnois was plundered and devastated by the English of Athlone; they took the large bells of the Cloicteach and left neither large nor small bell, image, altar, book, gem, nor even glass in a window in the walls of the church, that they did not carry away with them. The City of Ciaran, so often raped and ravaged, has also shown the recurring miracle of rebirth. At the very beginning there was nothing here but wooden, clay-and-wattle beehive huts. From what remains of the ancient ruins now seen at Clonmacnois one can imagine the splendour of what was there towards the end of its lifetime. Clonmacnois knew pillage and destruction, but it was also built up by generous benefactors and opened its doors to many distinguished and renowned visitors.

The ruins of old buildings in the monastic enclosure tell us something, but by no means all, about the long and chequered history of this sacred place. At the centre of the monastic buildings is the Eaglais Beag, the small church that is said to mark the burial place of St Ciaran. From this small church people have carried clay from St Ciaran's grave for centuries. The clay was spread on the fields as a protection against pests and diseases. The great Crosses, especially the Cross of the Scriptures, which are now indoors for safety, are a most impressive sight. There is one outstanding little building, the Nuns' Church, which is seen by few enough visitors to Clonmacnois because it is some distance from the main monastic ruins. It was saved and preserved in 1865 by Rev James Graves and the Kilkenny Archaeological Society.

The little that remains of Clonmacnois points to a very high standard of excellence in art work. The grave slabs, which are now carefully preserved indoors, are like pages of manuscripts with intricate interlacing patterns and lettering. The magnificent Shrine of St Manchan, now displayed in the Church of St Manchan at Boher, must, in its original beauty, have been a work of surpassing artistry.

For centuries people came to Clonmacnois on Pattern Day and did the 'long station'. This formula of prayer involved doing 'stations' or 'rounds' of the sacred site, often in bare feet. The station began at St Ciaran's Well, which is some distance from the monastic site on the road to Shannonbridge. The 'long station' was well named, for it truly took a long time to complete.

Clonmacnois is an impressive place for pilgrims and visitors. Of Clonmacnois, Dr John Healy, the historian, wrote a hundred years ago: 'Even still her churches, her crosses and her tombstones furnish the best and most characteristic specimens of the ancient Celtic art in sculpture and architecture. View it as you may, Clonmacnois was the greatest of our schools in the past, as it is the most interesting of our ruins at present'.

When Pope John Paul returned to Rome after his visit to Ireland in 1979, he said: 'I will never forget Clonmacnois as long as I live'.

Diocese of
Clogher

Most Rev Joseph Duffy DD

Born 3 February 1934 of Edward Duffy and Brigid MacEntee, Annagose, Newbliss, Co Monaghan, Joseph Duffy was educated at St Louis Infant School, Clones, Largy National School, Clones, and at St Macartan's College, Monaghan, where he was a boarder for five years. He studied for the priesthood at St Patrick's College, Maynooth, and was ordained a priest for the Diocese of Clogher on 22 June 1958. On 2 September 1979 he was ordained Bishop of Clogher.

After his ordination to the priesthood he continued his studies in Irish and completed a thesis on the dialect of south Tipperary for a Master's degree in the National University of Ireland in 1960. He then returned to St Macartan's College, where he taught Irish and French for twelve years. During these years he spent several sessions in French universities doing summer courses in French. He also worked at the pilgrimage shrine of Lough Derg in Co Donegal and translated two books of the Old Testament, Amos and Ezekiel, for *An Bíobla Naofa*.

From 1972 to 1979 he was a curate in the parish of Enniskillen, Co Fermanagh. This ministry included a chaplaincy to St Fanchea's College for girls and part-time chaplaincy to the Erne Hospital. During these years he was involved in PACE (Protestant and Catholic Encounter) and served on the committee of the Ulster Architectural Heritage Society.

His special interest outside his formal duties has been the local history of the Diocese of Clogher. From 1963 to 1975 he was editor and frequent contributor to *Clogher Record* and since 1975 he has been chairman of the Clogher Historical Society. In 1972 he published a popular work on St Patrick, *Patrick in his Own Words*, which is currently being revised.

As a member of the Bishops' Conference he was Episcopal Spokesman from 1987 to 1993 and has been Chairman of the Committee for European Affairs and delegate of the Conference on COMECE the Commission of Bishops' Conference of the European Community, since 1983 He has also been a member of the Inter-Church meeting, Chairman of the Episcopal Commission for Liturgy and Chairman of the Committee for Sacred Art and Architecture.

St Macartan's Cathedral, Monaghan

On Sunday, 3 January 1858, at a meeting of the Catholic inhabitants of the parish and vicinity of Monaghan, with the Bishop of Clogher, Dr Charles MacNally presiding, it was formally resolved that a new Catholic church at Monaghan was urgently required. An eight-acre site was purchased by the bishop from Humphrey Jones of Clontibret for £800, and an architect, James Joseph McCarthy of Dublin, was employed to draw a design

The style is French Gothic of the fourteenth century. In June 1861 the foundation stone was laid, and the work got underway the following year. Dr MacNally died in 1864, and work resumed under his successor, Dr James Donnelly, in 1865. The architect died in 1882 and was succeeded by William Hague, a Cavan man, who was responsible for the design of the spire and the gate-lodge. The work was completed in 1892, and the cathedral was solemnly dedicated on 21 August of that year.

Under the direction of the present bishop, Dr Joseph Duffy, a radical rearrangement and refurbishing of the interior of the cathedral was begun in 1982 to meet the requirements of the revised liturgy. The artist responsible for the general scheme was Michael Biggs of Dublin, in consultation with local architect Gerald MacCann. The altar is carved from a single piece of granite from south County Dublin. The sanctuary steps are in solid Travertine marble. The sanctuary crucifix is by

...ncludes County Monaghan, most of County Fermanagh, and parts of Counties Tyrone, Donegal, Louth and Cavan

...chard Enda King; the cross is of Irish
...k and the figure of Christ is cast in
...onze. The Lady Chapel has a bronze
...età by Nell Murphy, and the lettering
...the Magnificat is by Michael Biggs.
...he tabernacle, made of silver-plated
...eet bronze and mounted on a granite
...lar, has the form of a tent and was
...signed and made by Richard Enda
...ng. In the chapel of the Holy Oils the
...mbry was designed by Michael Biggs,
...ile the miniature bronze gates were
...ecuted by Martin Leonard. The five
...eat tapestries on the east walls of the
...thedral are a striking feature of the
...novation; they were designed by
...ances Biggs and woven by Terry
...unne, both of Dublin.

The Pietà

The Pietà in bronze (1989) was designed
by Nell Murphy for the Lady Chapel in
St Macartan's Cathedral. It shows a
courageous middle-aged Mary holding
her dead son and sharing the suffering of
the human race. It contains both the
strength and tenderness of the woman
portrayed in St John's Gospel.

Diocese of Clogher

HISTORY OF THE DIOCESE

THE CLOGHER VALLEY in south Tyrone was fertile ground for the seed that Patrick came to sow. Soon afterwards, to the west of this area, a cluster of monasteries sprang up along the shores and on the islands of Lough Erne. Among these were the monasteries of Clones and Devenish, which soon eclipsed Clogher, the place that Patrick had chosen as the see for his faithful *treanfhear* (strong man), Macartan.

But Patrick's choice was remembered and approved by the Synod of Rathbreasail in 1111. This synod fixed on Clogher as the see for a new diocese that would extend from the Blackwater river to Lough Erne, and from Slieve Larga, west of Omagh, to Slieve Beatha on the Monaghan-Fermanagh-Tyrone border. In time this small territory pushed out its boundaries to the south and the west. The Rathbreasail reform was taken up enthusiastically by a powerful local king, Donnchadh O'Carroll, with the result that the diocese kept extending eastwards as O'Carroll annexed the present county of Louth to his homeland in Monaghan. This expansion of the diocese was at the expense of the primatial see of Armagh and was approved by the great reformer St Malachy, a strange attitude even considering that Christian, the second bishop of Clogher, was Malachy's brother. For a time in the second half of the twelfth century the see moved from Clogher to the Abbey of Louth, where the bishop had his cathedral church and a chapter of Augustinian canons. Following the Norman invasion of Louth, the see returned to Clogher.

Meanwhile the same kind of expansion was happening in the west. This led to the incorporation of the extensive churchlands of Devenish south of Lower Lough Erne and the ancient kingdom of Toora, thus bringing the diocese to the sea at Bundoran before the year 1250. The political drive for this movement came from another powerful local sept, the Fir Manach, who were already establishing the new kingdom of Lough Erne at the time of Rathbreasail.

It was in this drive westwards that the diocese came to possess on its north-west border what was to become its most distinctive shrine. This became known throughout the Christian world as St Patrick's Purgatory, Lough Derg. As a national and international place of pilgrimage it goes back to at least the twelfth century. On several maps of the Renaissance period it is the sole Irish landmark. Some years ago it was discovered to be the inspiration of a fourteenth-century fresco in Todi in central Italy. It was of Lough Derg that Shane Leslie wrote: 'St Patrick's Purgatory was the medieval rumour which terrified travellers, awed the greatest of criminals, attracted the boldest of knight-errantry, puzzled the theologian, englamoured Ireland, haunted Europe, influenced the current views and doctrines of purgatory, and not least inspired Dante'. Whatever about this last-mentioned claim, the literature relating to the pilgrimage is extensive and stretches from medieval times to the present century, when two of our major poets, Patrick Kavanagh and Seamus Heaney, each chose it as a focus for an important poem.

The medieval period in the diocese was a time of learning and scholarship, of which we have many fine examples. In 1997 Professor Katherine Walsh of the University of Innsbruck, published, in *Clogher Record*, a fascinating account of a fourteenth-century Bishop of Clogher, John O'Corcoran, who was a distinguished graduate of the University of Prague. Another bishop, Piaras Maguire, was an Oxford canonist. There was also an Máistir Mór Ó hEoghain, a lecturer in Oxford. But the most eminent scholar of his time was undoubtedly Cathal Óg Mac Manus, the Dean of Lough Erne, who left us the famous *Annals of Ulster*. It is fitting that the Mac Manus clan around the world gathered to commemorate the fifth centenary of his death in 1498 at Cathal's native place, where he compiled his annals, the place now known as Belle Isle on Upper Lough Erne.

The Plantations of the seventeenth century brought total destruction and ruin to Catholic Church structures in Clogher as in the rest of Ireland. All diocesan lands and property were confiscated and clergy were subjected to the kind of regime we associate with Eastern Europe before the fall of the Berlin Wall. But the diocese was never without a number of young men who were ready to journey to France and Spain and the Low Countries for their education and return as priests. Nor should we forget the four Mac Mahon bishops who did honour to their name and calling in those dark days: Heber, Hugh, Bernard and Ross. The last three became Primates in Armagh. There is no better description of the operation of the Penal Laws than the account of the Diocese of Clogher sent to Rome in 1714.

The end of the eighteenth century brought a measure of toleration and saw the beginnings of the work of reconstruction. Modest 'Mass houses' were set up in backyards in the towns and inconspicuous sites in the country. This improving state of things was noted by Bishop James Murphy in 1804 in his report to Rome: 'Our illiterate laity, for nine tenths of our people owing to their great poverty are such, have made an astonishing progress in acquiring a competent knowledge of the Christian Doctrine within these few years back. This change has been effected by the zeal and exertions of the parish priests, many of whom have besides the public catechism established on Sunday mornings and evenings in their chapels and places of worship, prevailed with a number of the well-disposed laity to teach in the more remote parts of their parishes on Sunday evenings'. Dr Murphy set up a school in Monaghan to prepare young men for Maynooth. His successor, Dr Kernan, laid the foundation stone of the diocesan seminary in 1840, and Dr Kernan's successor, Dr MacNally, laid the foundation stone of St Macartan's Cathedral in 1861. Since then, unfortunately, the most significant development has been a negative one. The political settlement of 1922 left the diocese divided down the middle by a territorial border. This means that the current peace process has a relevance here as in few other parts of our country.

LACE OF PILGRIMAGE

Patrick's Purgatory, Lough Derg

Patrick's Purgatory is among the
dest centres of Christian Pilgrimage in
Vestern Europe, supposedly dating back
the sixth century. Its importance in
edieval times is indicated by the fact
at it was among the principal
ndmarks on maps of Ireland. It was, for
ample, the only Irish site named on a
orld map of 1492. The pilgrimage was
ry popular among Europeans at that
me and there are records of pilgrims
aving travelled from Hungary (1363 &
11), France (1325, 1397 & 1516), Italy
358 & 1411) and Holland (1411 & 1494).

The association of the name of St
atrick with Lough Derg dates back as far
records go and the legends that link him
ith the place point to a tradition already
mly established by the twelfth century.
While in a cave on the island, Patrick is said
have had a vision of the punishments of
ell. Hence the place came to be known as
Patrick's Purgatory.

Each year the traditional three-day
lgrimage begins on 1 June and ends on
August. Pilgrims must be at least fifteen
ars of age, in good health and able to
alk and kneel unaided. The pilgrimage
a three-day fast incorporating a 24-hour
gil. Pilgrims arrive on the island
tween 11.00 am and 3.00 pm, having
sted from the previous midnight. They
ve one simple meal of dry toast,
tcakes and black tea or coffee on each of
e three days. The central prayer of the
lgrimage is called a 'station'. Each

station involves the repeated praying of
the Our Father, the Hail Mary and the
Apostles' Creed, as pilgrims walk or kneel
or stand, barefooted. The greater part of a
station is made on the Penitential Beds.
(These are thought to be the remnants of
beehive cells used by the early monks.)
Three such stations are made on the first
day. Four more stations are made in
common in the Basilica during the night
vigil and one is made on each of the
second and third days.

In former times the emphasis was
more on the physical penance and
hardship of the pilgrimage exercises.
Nowadays those who make the pilgrimage
see it as a grace-filled opportunity to get
away from the stress of modern-day
living. They talk about the cleansing value
of fasting and see the intensive and
concentrated nature of the routine as
giving opportunities for prioritising values
and being physically and spiritually
renewed. They find that the particular
prayer-form, which they often refer to as
'body-prayer', is very satisfying and
expresses in a non-verbal way what they
often cannot put into words.

Walking barefooted serves to
emphasise what all have in common and
creates a greater awareness of community.
This is particularly effective in the
celebration of liturgies on the island. The
Sacrament of Reconciliation has always
been, and still is, very central to this
penitential pilgrimage. Its celebration
each morning in the Basilica is a moment
of joy and hope for penitents and priests
alike. However, it is the Eucharist that
most pilgrims experience as the high

point of their pilgrimage. The liturgy of
the Roman Missal is given full expression,
with excellent response from pilgrims.
Young people have key roles in the
welcoming and music ministries.

Throughout the season pilgrims are
offered opportunities for spiritual
direction and a counselling service is
provided for any who wish to avail of it.

The pilgrimage fee is IR£20.00 (or
sterling equivalent) and includes boat
fare and accommodation. Pilgrims leave
the island by 10.00 am on the third day
of their pilgrimage and continue their
fast until midnight. Warm and
waterproof clothing is advisable.

One-Day Retreats were introduced
at Lough Derg in 1992. The retreats are
particularly suited to those who for
various reasons cannot make the Three-
Day Pilgrimage. These are structured
days of prayer and contemplation and do
not entail fasting or walking barefooted,
and pilgrims are invited to celebrate the
Sacrament of Reconciliation. The day
finishes with a celebration of Eucharist.
Each retreat begins at 10.00 am and ends
at approx. 5.00 pm. (Boats run
continuously from 9.15 am until 10.30
am.) The Retreats cost IR£12.00 (or
sterling equivalent) per person, and
include boat fare, coffee and a light
lunch. It is essential to make a
reservation by letter or telephone. For
bookings telephone/ fax 072-61518
during office hours. Email:
lochderg@iol.ie. Visit the website
www.iol.ie/~loch derg or write to: The
Prior, St Patrick's Purgatory, Lough
Derg, Pettigo, Co Donegal.

Diocese of
Clonfert

Most Rev John Kirby DD

Bishop John Kirby is a native of Athlone and was born in 1938. He was educated at the local Convent National School, Dean Kelly Boys' National School and St Joseph's College, Garbally, Ballinasloe. He entered St Patrick's College, Maynooth, in 1956 and was ordained to the priesthood in June 1963.

Later that year, he was appointed to teach mathematics in Garbally. When the then President of the college, Fr Joe Cassidy, was appointed Coadjutor Bishop of Clonfert in 1979, Fr Kirby succeeded as President. In 1987 Bishop Cassidy was transferred to become Archbishop of Tuam, and Fr Kirby was appointed Bishop of Clonfert in February 1988 and was ordained in April.

Currently, Bishop Kirby is Chairman of Trócaire, the development agency established by the Irish Catholic Bishops in 1973. He is also a member of the Episcopal Commission for Clergy, Vocations and Seminaries and is the contact bishop for Faith & Light, a group following the ideals of Jean Vanier, which cares for the needs of handicapped people and their families.

St Brendan's Cathedral, Loughrea

St Brendan's Cathedral stands at the western extremity of the Diocese of Clonfert on the main highway from Dublin to Galway. The foundation stone of the cathedral was laid on 10 October 1897, and the fabric was completed in 1902. Plans were drawn by the Dublin architect William Byrne for a building in the neo-Gothic style, having a nave and an aspidal sanctuary, lean-to aisles and shallow transepts, with a graceful spire at the western end. Its dimensions were determined by the needs of the parish of Loughrea. While not impressive, its proportions are good, and despite a departure from the original plan by curtailment of the sanctuary, the overall effect is pleasing. The simplicity of the exterior, however, hardly prepares the visitor for the riches within.

It was due to two fortuitous circumstances

that St Brendan's became a veritable treasure house of the Celtic Revival in sculpture, stained glass, woodcarving, metalwork and textiles.

The first circumstance was that the building of a Catholic cathedral was delayed for various reasons until close to the turn of the last century. The Irish Literary Renaissance was by then well advanced. When the building was completed in 1902, the Arts and Crafts movement was having effect.

The second circumstance was that of Edward Martyn's birth at the home of his maternal grandfather, James Smyth, in the parish of Loughrea. Martyn was an ascetic man and devoted his time and fortune to the development of every phase of the Irish revival, the Gaelic League, Sinn Féin, the Irish Literary Theatre, Irish music, church music and church art. With innate business acumen he insured by personal donation and the financial support of the Smyth family that the new cathedral would reflect his views. The bishop, Dr John Healy, who was sensitive to the prevailing trend, accepted the challenge and assigned the project to the supervision of a young curate in the parish, Fr Jeremiah O'Donovan, who was himself actively engaged in propaganda for Revival.

John Hughes was the foremost sculptor in the country at the time, and Bishop Healy commissioned him to do the modelling and carving. His work is found in the bronze figure of Christ on the reredos of the high altar and in the magnificent marble statue of the Virgin and Child. Michael Shortall, a student of Hughes in the Metropolitan School of Art, did the carvings on the corbels and executed the statue of St Brendan on the wall of the tower. His connection with the cathedral continued over twenty years, and he was responsible for carving of incidents from the life and voyage of St Brendan carved on the capitals of the pillars.

The Yeats sisters, Lily and Elizabeth, along with their friend Evelyn Gleeson, set up the Dun Emer guild. They

nbroidered twenty-four banners of ish saints for use in the cathedral. Jack Yeats and his wife Mary designed ese banners. With an economy of etail and richness of colour, they almost hieve the effect of stained glass. Mass stments, embroidered with silk on plin, also came from the same studio.

ore than anything else, St Brendan's is mous for its stained glass. Martyn was rticularly concerned about the quality stained glass then available in Ireland. e was eager to set up an Irish stained-ass industry. He succeeded in having fred E. Childe appointed to the etropolitan School of Art, and he later rsuaded Sarah Purser to open a co-erative studio, where young artists uld be trained in the technique of ined glass. This new studio, An Túr oinne, opened in January 1903, with hilde as manager, and so began the ork of the Loughrea stained-glass ndows. Over the next forty years, hilde, Purser and Michael Healy ecuted almost all the stained-glass ndows in the cathedral, and it is these ndows that have given St Brendan's its ace in the Irish Artistic Revival.

St John the Evangelist, stained-glass window, St Brendan's Cathedral

Michael Healy designed and painted ten stained-glass windows in St Brendan's Cathedral. That depicting St Simeon was Healy's first complete window. This detailed drawing displays his debt to the Renaissance, but also the fact that he had not yet mastered the stained-glass technique. In 1907 he was commissioned to design and paint two rose windows over the side altars. Healy designed, painted and completed his St John the Evangelist window in 1927. This window shows extraordinary development from his early work at Loughrea. The apocalyptic figure of the saint, youthful and beardless, almost fills the window, while in a small panel below he appears as an aged man writing the Gospel. The dramatic colour effect is enhanced by the 'aciding' technique, which he developed and used so extensively in his later windows.

Healy went on to produce six more spectacular windows: Christ the King (1930); Queen of Heaven (1933); Kilcorban Madonna; St Joseph (1935); the Ascension (1936) and the Last Judgement (1937-40).

Diocese of
Clonfert

HISTORY OF THE DIOCESE

Like most dioceses in Ireland, the Diocese of Clonfert had its origin in the Synod of Rathbreasail in 1111, reaching its final form at the Synod of Kells in 1152. Before that, the early Irish monastery and school of Clonfert was the dominant ecclesiastical centre in the area. It nestled close to the river Shannon on its western bank and its *paruchia* intermingled with that of Clonmacnois. Despite the vicissitudes of these early centuries its fame grew and the annals record, apart from bishops, abbots and coarbs of the founder, Brendan, the names of numbers of scribes, lectors, anchorites and *'fir-leighin'*, who laboured and prayed and studied there. It was also deeply involved in the eight-century spiritual reform movement of the 'Céili Dé'.

St Brendan's fame as a seafaring missionary contributed to its pre-eminence in later times and led to its choice as an episcopal see in the twelfth century. He was held in reverence from Brittany to the far-off Faroes. It must have been this established reputation that caused his name to be attached to the medieval tale, the 'Voyage of Brendan', which made its way into the literatures of Europe and led to later voyages of discovery.

Territorially, the modern diocese occupies almost the whole of East Galway, with one parish, Lusmagh in Co Offaly and Taughmaconnell as well as Creagh, the half-parish of Ballinasloe, in Co Roscommon. This was the ancient territory of Hy Many, the largest petty-kingdom in the country, as it existed when the diocese was formed. In fact, its bishop was sometimes referred to as the Bishop of Hy Many.

Clonfert cathedral, the nave of which is twelfth-century or earlier, still stands, and its western doorway, supreme example of the Hiberno-Romanesque style, is on architectural grounds assigned a date of about 1180. The place had been burned in 1179. Before that one of the important events of the Twelfth Century

Reform took place there. As the *Annals of Clonmacnois* described it: 'In the year 1170 there was a great convocation of the clergy of Ireland at Clonfert by commission from the Pope for the reformation of certain abuses of a long time used in Ireland'. St Laurence O'Toole presided there as Papal legate.

The diocese was divided into four deaneries, Clonfert, Loughrea, Urrachree and Duniry, having fifteen rectories and thirty-nine vicarages, with a chapter and offices after the Norman pattern. Four houses of canons regular and four of canonesses were established in the Irish deaneries.

Bishops of the diocese, in the fourteenth and fifteenth centuries, introduced mendicant orders – Franciscans to Kilconnell, Kilnalahan and Meelick, with their 3rd Order to Clonkeenkerril and Kilbocht; Dominicans to Portumna, with their 3rd Order to Kilcorban and Carmelites to Loughrea. The Canons disappeared with the Reformation, but the mendicants remained to become an important factor in maintaining religion during the penal times, until, with the establishment of Maynooth College in 1795, the flow of secular priests became adequate again. Evading the law by registering as parish priests in 1704, they served one-third of the parishes throughout the eighteenth century.

Forty-one parishes in 1704 were by the year 1800 amalgamated into twenty-four, with little change to the present time. The chapter disappeared after Emancipation, when an era of church building began, which replaced the poor structures of the penal times and included such worthy churches as those at Ballymacward and Ballinasloe, the latter designed by McCarthy and Pugin. Landlord intransigence prevented the building of a cathedral in Loughrea until 1897, when Bishop Healy laid the foundation stone, which was fortunate because the era of the Celtic Revival and Irish stained glass had begun, with happy results in its interior decoration.

The Sisters of Mercy were brought to Loughrea in 1850 by Bishop Derry and spread to five towns in the diocese,

operating primary and secondary schools, industrial schools at Loughrea and Ballinasloe and a domestic economy school at Portumna. They also staffed the workhouse hospitals in Loughrea, Ballinasloe and Portumna and, latterly, the county home in Loughrea. The Sisters of Mount Carmel, who have been in Loughrea since the seventeenth century, conducted a school there up to 1860 but have since been an enclosed order. In 1945 Bishop Dignan introduced the Franciscan Missionaries of the Divine Motherhood to Ballinasloe, where they built Portiuncula Hospital, which has been enlarged many times since and is now a general hospital under the Western Health Board.

The diocesan seminary, begun at Loughrea by Bishop Derry in the last century, was succeeded by St Joseph's College at Cartron, at Esker, and finally at Garbally Park since 1924. The Dominicans, who had come from Athenry, ran a college at Esker for a time, where now the Redemptorists have a house for retreats.

PLACE OF PILGRIMAGE

'The Friary', Abbey

About eight miles west of Portumna is the village of Abbey in the foothills of the Sliabh Aughty Mountains. The ruin in the centre of the village, known locally as 'The Friary', are all that remains of a unique religious foundation dating from the mid thirteenth century.

Following the arrival of the Norman in Ireland in 1169, many of the French and German orders set up foundations here. The Carthusians established a monastery at Kilnalahan or Kinelechin (Cineál Fheichin, the tribe of Feichin) the Diocese of Clonfert about 1252. The community was small and did not develop to any great extent; the monks departed from the monastery about 133 and the house lay derelict for a number of years.

Pope Gregory IX granted a bull to the Franciscans enabling them to take over the monastery, and the friars arrived in Kilnalahan in 1371. The community was again a small one but they developed strong roots in the area. In 1400 Pope Boniface granted an indulgence to those who visited the friary and gave alms for its maintenance and repair.

As it did not have much in the way of land, the friary was not worth confiscating following the Reformation. However, in the unsettled period at the end of the 1500s it was destroyed. It was rebuilt in 1615 and for a while Michael O'Clery, one of the 'Four Masters', lived and studied there. The friars were again dispersed during the Cromwellian period, but returned as soon as the trouble subsided.

The introduction of the Penal Laws in 1695 was the beginning of the end for the abbey. The friars were banished from the country and though some filtered back to the district in 1712 they were unable to occupy the abbey itself. They struggled on for a time, but by 1800 there is no evidence of the friars in the area.

Because of this long history, the Bishop of Clonfert has designated 'The Friary' in Abbey as the venue for pilgrimage in this Jubilee Year 2000.

Diocese of
Cloyne

Cloyne

Most Rev John Magee DD

John Magee was born on 24 September 1936 in Newry, Co Down. His parents were Charles and Agnes Magee (née Breslin). He attended primary school at the Abbey, Christian Brothers, Newry, and received his secondary education at St Colman's College, Newry. In September 1954 he entered the Missionary Society of St Patrick (Kiltegan Fathers). From 1955 to 1958 he studied in UCC, graduating with a BA degree. The next four years saw him in Rome, where he was conferred with an STL from the Lateran University in 1962.

On 17 March 1962, in St John's Lateran Basilica, Rome, John Magee was ordained to the priesthood for the Kiltegan Fathers. He spent the next six years in Ireland, first as principal of a training college and then of a secondary school. In 1968 he returned to Rome as Procurator General of the Kiltegans, and from 1969 to 1975 he was a member of the Congregation for the Propagation of the Faith. He was appointed Private Secretary in succession to Pope Paul VI, Pope John Paul I and Pope John Paul II, until 1982, when he was appointed Master of Pontifical Ceremonies.

He was consecrated Bishop of Cloyne by Pope John Paul II on 17 March 1987, the position he currently holds. From July 1994 to March 1996, he also acted as Apostolic Administrator of Limerick. From 1992 to 1997, Bishop Magee served as a member of the Congregation for Bishops. He is Chairman of the Irish Episcopal Commissions for Liturgy, for Missions and for Religious.

St Colman's Cathedral, Cobh

St Colman's Cathedral, overlooking Cobh, enshrines within its walls the traditions of thirteen centuries of the Diocese of Cloyne.

Built in the form of a Latin cross, its exterior is of Dalkey granite, with dressings of Mallow limestone. The style of architecture is French Gothic. The architects were Pugin (the Younger), Ashlin and Coleman.

The cathedral took forty-seven years to build (1868-1915). The total cost was £235,000. Of this, £90,000 was raised by the people of Cobh, with the remainder coming from the diocese and from collections in America and Australia.

The spire was completed in 1915 and the famous carillon and the clock were installed in 1916. The carillon – the largest in Britain and Ireland – has forty-nine bells and is tuned to the accuracy of a single vibration. This unusual instrument covers a range of four octaves and is played from a console located in the belfry, consisting of a keyboard and pedalboard. Inside, the cathedral has all the hallmarks of Gothic grandeur: the massive marble pillars, the beautiful arches, the capitals with their delicate carving of foliage, the shamrock design on the Bath Stone, and mellow, delicate lighting.

The carved panels over the nave arches give a history of the Church in Ireland from the time of St Patrick. The stained glass windows in the northern aisle depict the parables of Christ, while those in the southern aisle depict the miracles of Christ. Overhead, in the clerestory, are forty-six windows, each having the patron of one of the forty-six parishes of the diocese. The high altar and its surround was designed by Ashlin. The pulpit is of Austrian oak. Towards the rear of the cathedral is the magnificent rose window, which depicts St John's vision of the throne of God. The organ was built by Telford and Telford, and has a total of 2,468 pipes

The South Transept, St Colman's Cathedral

The South Transept, in glass and stone, tells the story of the Redeemer's work of salvation. It begins in the line of windows.

In the centre window, God is represented as he was spoken of in the Old Testament: 'The Almighty', 'The Lawgiver', 'The God of Justice'.

On either side of this window are three lights showing some of the figures raised up by God to prepare humankind for the great revelation of the New Testament. On the left is Naaman, who washed seven times in the Jordan and was cleansed of leprosy. In the next window, Eliseus is shown receiving the mantle of Elias. In the third window, Josue leads the chosen people into the Promised Land.

The fifth window shows Moses leading the chosen people out of Egypt and across the Red Sea. The sixth window shows the sacrifice of Noah after the deluge, and the seventh shows the sacrifice of Melchisedech.

The windows were designed by Hardman of Birmingham.

Diocese of Cloyne

HISTORY OF THE DIOCESE

St colman, patron of the Diocese of Cloyne, was the son of Lenin (he was known as Mac Lenin) and was reputed to be of royal stock. He was born about 522 in Muskerry, a vast area that may have included Kilmaclenine, which could have been the birthplace of the saint. Brought up in heathenism, he studied for twelve years to become a bard, and eventually became the Royal Bard of Munster, which made him historian, genealogist, geographer and chronicler to the Munster kings in Cashel.

He was involved in the discovery of the Shrine of St Ailbe of Emly, which had been stolen, and St Brendan decreed that Mac Lenin, having touched the sacred shrine, should not defile himself with heathen practices but should become a Christian. He changed his original name to Colman, resigned his position as bard, studied under St Jarlath of Tuam and was eventually ordained a priest.

His principal foundation was at Cloyne, Cluain Uamha, 'Meadow of the Caves', where he founded the monastery and the great school of Cloyne. He was given land also at Kilmaclenine, near Buttevant, by the kings of Munster.

St Colman died about the year 604, on 24 November, which is observed as his feastday. The profound influence of his spiritual mission was endorsed when he was canonised by popular acclaim.

CLOYNE – CLUAIN UAMHA

Cluain Uamha was one of the royal seats of the kings of Cashel. In 580 Cairpre Crom granted Cloyne to St Colman as a site for his monastery. According to the Irish Annals, the Danes raided the monastery three times, in 822, 824 and 885. In the third raid the abbot and prior were murdered. The men of Ossory plundered Cloyne in 978 and Diarmuid O'Brien devasted it in 1088.

A great restoration of monasteries took place when Brian Boru began to get the upper hand on the Danes. The round tower of Cloyne was built about the year 1000, half stronghold, half belfry. It was struck by lightning on 10 January 1747; the roof was destroyed and the bell thrown down.

Even the Danish attacks indicated that the monastery of Cloyne flourished and was worth plundering. The monastery was a very important unit of society. Around an Irish monastery, crafts of all kinds were practised, which meant employment for people. The monks provided for the religious needs not only of those living near the monastery but of those at centres far removed from it. Subsequent diocesan development indicates that the sphere of influence of the monastery of Cloyne extended to a big part of County Cork.

THE DIOCESE OF CLOYNE

About 1100, an effort was made to reform the Church and bring it into line with the Church in Rome and on the Continent, where Church organisation was episcopal. In 1152 the Synod of Kells divided the country into four provinces with four archbishops. The monastic district of Cloyne now became the Diocese of Cloyne. The boundaries of each diocese were drawn at Kells, and soon afterwards it became necessary to establish the exact boundaries of each parish.

THE PIPE ROLL OF CLOYNE

The changeover to diocesan organisation did not mean the end of monasteries in Ireland. In fact, many new monasteries were founded in the twelfth century. The Cistercian monastery of Midleton was founded in 1180 and flourished for 361 years. After the arrival of the Normans in 1169 Norman names occur among the bishops of Cloyne. Nicholas de Effingham was Bishop of Cloyne from 1284 to 1320 and Bishop John de Swafham, another Englishman, ruled the diocese from 1363 until 1367. De Swafham made an effort to found diocesan archives. He assembled whatever documents he could find and had them copied on parchment (sheep-skin). The documents concerned the possessions of the diocese, the tenants of diocesan lands, the bishop's revenue and other rights. These were sewn together to form a long scroll. Other documents were attached later, until the roll measured seventeen feet in length. This is known as the Pipe Roll of Cloyne. Transactions that took place during the episcopacies of eleven Cloyne bishops were mentioned from David McKelly 1227 to Alan Pay 1423.

DIOCESE OF CLOYNE (15TH-17TH CENTURY)

The Dioceses of Cork and Cloyne were united by Papal Decree under Bishop Jordan Purcell in 1432 and remained so united until 1747. About 1540 the monasteries of Cloyne diocese were suppressed and their lands were given to laymen. In 1558 Elizabeth 1 became queen and Protestantism became the State religion. By 1588 Cloyne cathedral had passed into the hands of the Reformers. By 1615 most of the parish churches of the diocese were in ruins. After the 1641 rebellion Cloyne cathedral was again in Catholic hands and Mass was celebrated in it for five years. By 1651 Cromwell's conquest of Ireland was complete. Persecution of Catholics followed. In 1698 Catholic bishops, VGs, deans, Jesuits and monks were ordered to leave the country and many Penal Laws were enacted.

THE PENAL ERA IN CLOYNE

During penal times clerical students had to go secretly to the Irish Colleges on the Continent and newly ordained priests had to re-enter the country in secret. The Irish College at Toulouse was virtually a seminary for the Dioceses of Cork, Cloyne and Ross. It was suppressed in 1789.

According to the Annals, 'The diocesan fabric was alarmingly run down in 1731. This was the age of Mass-rocks and miserable open-ended Mass-houses. The majority of the priests were 'on the run'. There seems to have been considerable improvement over the years 1731-1764. Of the seventy-one chapels mentioned for Cloyne Diocese in the Hearth Money Returns for 1764, only four are described as being in bad order. But even at this stage and for many more years the standard would have been very low'.

CLOYNE DIOCESE (19TH-20TH CENTURY)

The nineteenth century witnessed great progress, with convents, monasteries and schools being founded all over the diocese, and many priests and religious departing to work in all five Continents. The great age of church-building dawned shortly before 1800 with the building of St Mary's Church, Youghal, and gradually new parish churches were built throughout the diocese. The most ambitious project began in 1867 when Bishop William Keane undertook the building of St Colman's Cathedral, Cobh. On 12 August 1919, the cathedral, built at a cost of £235,000, was consecrated by Bishop Robert Browne. Bishop John Magee has undertaken massive renovations, now nearing completion, to prepare St Colman's Cathedral to enter the third millennium.

PLACE OF PILGRIMAGE

Shrine of St Gobnet, Ballyvourney

One of the approximate dates given for the religious foundation of St Gobnet at Ballyvourney is 650. Some would give an earlier date. The genealogists speak of Gobnet as being of the race of Conaire Mór. She is said to have set out on her journey to Ballyvourney from Inish Thiar (Aran Islands), having come hence from Clare. The story goes that she had a vision in which she was told that she was to make a religious foundation at the place where she would find nine white deer grazing together. Connacht and Munster claim holy spots that mark her sojourn or residence. Among the places at which she stopped on her wanderings were Ballyagran (Co Limerick), Kilgobnet near Dungarvan and Kilgobnet near Lombardstown. There were religious foundations in her honour at these places.

At Cillin na bFiadhan (in Ballyvourney parish), she crossed the Sullane and found the nine white deer. Here she founded her cell, and Teampall Gobnatan became the religious centre of Muscraidhe Uí Fhloinn. (Muscraidhe Uí Fhloinn was a district extending from An Dribseach to Buirneach, i.e. from the river Dripsey to Ballyvourney). It was the territory of Flann. Ua Floinn was said to have had his chief residence at Magh Cromtha.

Tradition tells of her solicitude for the people of the district, especially for the poor. A convent of nuns grew up about her. Later years saw larger and more substantial buildings erected. In Kerry there are many places associated with the name of St Gobnet. Her cult became widespread in the South, though we need not believe that she visited every place associated with her name.

St Gobnet's cult has been long and historic. Her greatest recognition by the Church came in 1601, when Pope Clement VIII, the ardent supporter of the Catholic Irish in their fight against the Reformers, imparted a special indulgence to those who would visit the parish church of St Gobnet on her feastday and who would fulfil the conditions of prayer, go to confession and receive Holy Communion.

St Gobnet's convent is no longer in Ballyvourney, but the saint's help remains. Crowds of people come on her feastday, 11 February, and also on Whitsunday. Perhaps the custom of 'doing rounds' on 11 February commenced soon after the saint's death. The 'round' takes over one hour to complete, during which time eighty-seven Paters, eighty-seven Aves and fifteen Credos are recited. A memory of the old pagan idea that wells and rivers have spirits that manifest themselves in the form of fish is preserved in the local belief that, if the request of the pilgrim is to be granted, a trout appears in the well as the pilgrim completes the 'round'.

In 1950 the Ballyvourney people decided to erect a statue to their saint at the old church and graveyard on the hillside. In doing so, they excavated an overgrown mound that was traditionally said to be St Gobnet's house or 'Kitchen'. Excavation revealed the walls of a round stone house that had been roofed with thatch and that was very probably the saint's house. A well was found outside the door.

St Gobnet's grave at Ballyvourney

Dioceses of
Cork and Ross

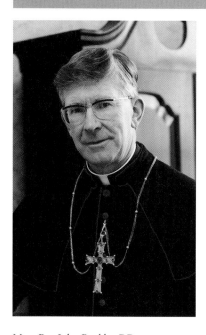

Most Rev John Buckley DD

Bishop Buckley was born in Inchigeela (Uibh Laoire parish) in west Cork on 2 November 1939.

After attending the local national school, he studied at St Finbarr's Seminary, Farranferris, Cork and at St Patrick's College, Maynooth. He was ordained a priest of the Cork diocese in 1965.

His first appointment was to the teaching staff of St Finbarr's Seminary, Farranferris. He was appointed President of Farranferris in 1976.

In July 1983 he was appointed Parish Priest of Turner's Cross parish in Cork city. He was ordained Auxiliary Bishop of Cork and Ross on 29 April 1984 at the cathedral.

Bishop Buckley was elected Diocesan Administrator after the death of Bishop Michael Murphy, who died on 7 October 1996. His appointment as Bishop of Cork and Ross was announced on 19 December 1997. He was installed as Bishop of Cork and Ross at a ceremony in the Cathedral of St Mary and St Anne, Cork, on Sunday, 8 February 1998.

Cathedral of St Mary and St Anne, Cork

The first cathedral on the site of the present Cathedral of St Mary and St Anne was the vision of Bishop Francis Moylan, who was Bishop of Cork from 1887 to 1915. The foundation stone was laid in 1799 and the cathedral was opened in 1808 as the parish church of the single parish then on the northside of the city – hence its local, popular name: the North Chapel. But in June 1820, the heat of the political climate struck the North Chapel when it was maliciously burned during the night.

Bishop John Murphy, one of the famous brewing family, wasted no time in calling a meeting to help restore the cathedral. The people of Cork generously rallied to the call.

The task of rebuilding was given to architect George Pain, who later designed Blackrock Castle, the court-house and St Patrick's Church. The interior of the present-day cathedral, including the ornate ceiling, owes much to his creative gifts.

The next major alteration to the cathedral was undertaken in the 1870s when Canon Foley set about building the tower and the great Western Door – now the main door of the cathedral. The tower is higher than that of its more famous neighbour: St Anne's Church, Shandon, home of the much-played bells.

Almost a hundred years later, after the Second Vatican Council, Cornelius Lucey, then Bishop of Cork and Ross, added a further major extension at the other end of the cathedral. This included a completely new sanctuary and a smaller tower, and added capacity to the church which served an area with a rapidly increasing population.

In 1994, major problems were discovered in the roof and other fabric of the building, which led to the closing of the cathedral for major refurbishment. The bishop, Michael Murphy, decided it was time to renovate the interior of the cathedral too. The task was entrusted to architect Richard Hurley, whose plan for the new interior saw a greater unity being achieved between the sanctuary and the rest of the floor area, and the new altar occupying the central place of prominence. The reordering and renovation was completed in 1996 at a cost of £2.5m and Bishop Murphy presided over its rededication – his last public function before he died a week later.

1 líontaióh óé go gcastar sinn

Altar, St Brigid's Church, Ballydehob

St Brigid's Church, Ballydehob (in the parish of Schull) has what may be one of the heaviest altars in the land! A rock was taken from a local beach and integrated into the reordered sanctuary. No masonry work was required. The natural proportions of the rock lend themselves in shape and height to being the central focus as the people gather to be nourished by the Giver of all.

Diocese of Cork includes Cork city and a portion of County Cork. Diocese of Ross includes part of County Cork

Cork and Ross

Dioceses of
Cork and Ross

HISTORY OF THE DIOCESES

THE UNITED dioceses of Cork and Ross include Cork city, west Cork and most of mid Cork on the south side of the river Lee. The dioceses also extend eastward to Glounthaune and north-east to Watergrasshill.

The Diocese of Ross is comprised of eleven parishes on the seaboard stretching from Timoleague, near Clonakilty, to Aughadown, west of Skibbereen. It includes parishes with beaches that are well known to holiday-makers from near and far. Places like Inchdoney, Baltimore and Owenahincha are all under the patronage of St Fachtna. The diocese also includes several islands, including the Gaeltacht of Oileán Cléire and Sherkin Island, which has earned a name for study and research of its maritime environment.

Ross diocese enjoyed complete independence between the twelfth century (when most diocesan boundaries were agreed) and 1693, when it was united with Cork and Cloyne. In 1849 it regained its own diocesan bishop, until it was united with Cork diocese in 1954.

Ross is predominantly a rural diocese, and the rural community accounts for a sizable part of the Cork diocese, too. However, Cork city and its suburbs, the country's second largest urban area, is home to the majority of the people of Cork diocese.

Cork diocese has at different times been joined with Ross and Cloyne, including a period of 320 years from 1429 when it was joined with the latter.

The border of the diocese is aligned with the valley of the river Lee, which flows into the sea at Cork but rises near Gougane Barra, in the parish of Inchigeela. The heart of this popular pilgrimage and wedding site is the Oratory of St Finbarr, patron of the Diocese of Cork, to whom tradition attributes the foundation of a monastic settlement in the marshlands of Cork, from which the city later evolved. The Lee, famed in anthem and story, also

provides an approximate guide to the line between Cloyne and Cork dioceses.

The Cathedral of St Mary and St Anne overlooks the city from the north side and is the diocesan see. A complete renovation of the historic cathedral was initiated in 1994 by the late Bishop Michael Murphy. The work, including a reordering of the interior, was completed in 1996 at a cost of £2.5m. The cathedral, which is known in the north side of the city as the North Chapel, has served the people for almost two hundred years. The people of the cathedral parish have been assisted by others from all parts of the dioceses and from far away in meeting the costs involved in the renovations, which will ensure its future as a worthy host to sacred moments in the lives of its congregations. The cathedral is also where Bishop John Buckley began his ministry as bishop of the dioceses on 8 February 1998. Like Finbarr, Bishop Buckley is from Inchigeela parish and was auxiliary bishop since 1984.

The Dioceses of Cork and Ross are known for a strong spirit of mission. Cork city is home to the Presentation Sisters, founded by Nano Nagle in the heart of the city at the beginning of the last century. Religious sisters and brothers of many congregations have moulded much of the life of the dioceses and their contribution has been enormous, especially in health and education.

People have also left from here to dot the globe with their own special imprint of Christianity. Missionary societies, religious orders and congregations are to be found at nearly every crossroads in the city and surrounding country. Their work is intertwined with the life and spirit of the people and the place.

The local dioceses also have a special connection with Peru and Ecuador in South America. The dioceses are spiritually twinned with 150,000 people in a shanty-town on the outskirts of the city of Trujillo in northern Peru. This link goes back to the 1960s when priests and religious from Cork took pastoral responsibility for the area. Since then many of the priests of the dioceses and hundreds of Mercy and Bon

Secours sisters have spent time working on the mission.

A second mission was established on the edge of the city of Manta in Ecuador in 1992. The parishes have 80,000 people who are also served by Cork and Ross priests. The work in both cities has involved everything from providing health centres, to school classrooms, to catechetics programmes, to building churches, to helping people to work together for their own development.

Modern-day Cork and Ross, with its pioneering pharmaceutical industries, computer plants, centres of learning, gourmet restaurants and advanced factories, continues to provide a challenging place to live the Christian life.

LACE OF PILGRIMAGE

he Oratory, Gougane Barra

he river Lee springs from the heart of
ibh Laoire parish in west Cork, on the
orders between Cork and Kerry. In its
rly meanderings it flows through a lake
Gougane Barra, near Ballingeary,
hich has long been a favourite place of
lgrimage and relaxation.

Saint Finbarr, patron of the Diocese
Cork and of the city of Cork,
tablished a monastic settlement on a
nall island on the lake in the era of
ints and scholars'. He is said to have
avelled along the banks of the river Lee
nd established a further site where the
ver meets the sea, around which grew
e city of Cork. The gates of the Honan
hapel at University College Cork
oclaim to visitors: 'Where Finbarr
ught, let Munster learn'.

Finbarr's feastday is on 25
ptember. On the Sunday nearest the
te, people from across the dioceses
ngregate at the oratory that now stands
ar his original settlement to mark
ougane Sunday'. The oratory is also a
vourite place for the celebration of the
crament of Marriage. Thousands of
uples have pledged themselves in
arriage to the gentle sound of the
ling waters of Lock Allua.

Diocese of
Derry

Most Rev Séamus Hegarty DD

Bishop Hegarty was born in January 1940 in Kilcar, Co Donegal. He was the eldest of three children of the late Mr and Mrs James Hegarty.

Educated at Kilcar National School and St Eunan's College, Letterkenny, he studied for the priesthood at St Patrick's College, Maynooth, where he obtained a BA degree in Theology and Celtic Studies.

Ordained for the Diocese of Raphoe in June 1966, he was awarded a Higher Diploma in Education with Honours at UCD in 1967. Bishop Hegarty then joined the teaching staff of Holy Cross College at Falcarragh, Co Donegal, where he was Dean of Studies until his appointment as President in 1971. In 1973, with the rationalisation of education in the north west, a community school – Pobalscoil Chloich Cheannfhaola – was set up and Bishop Hegarty was appointed Principal.

In August 1981 he was appointed curate at Stranorlar, Co Donegal. However, his sojourn there was to last only a few months, until his appointment as Bishop of Raphoe the following February. His ordination as Bishop took place on 28 March 1982 in St Eunan's Cathedral, Letterkenny.

He is a native Irish speaker and also speaks German fluently.

He was appointed Bishop of Derry on 1 October 1994 and installed on 6 November 1994.

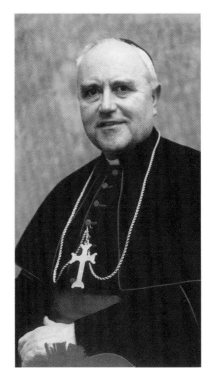

St Eugene's Cathedral, Derry

In the 1830s, following the Catholic Emancipation Act of 1829, the Catholic community of Derry was able to contemplate building a cathedral. In the summer of 1838, a number of Catholics of the city met with the then Bishop of Derry, Peter McLaughlin, to consider such a project. Over the next thirteen years a weekly collection was made in the city and eventually, on 26 July 1851, the foundation stone was laid by Bishop Francis Kelly.

The construction of the cathedral was sporadic as the funds became available over twenty-five years, and owing to the difficulty in raising money, it was agreed to postpone the building of the tower, belfry and spire until a later date. Due to the lack of funds in the diocese, the windows were initially all of plain glass, and it was only in later years that the stained glass was installed.

J. J. McCarthy (1817-82) was the architect commissioned to design St Eugene's Cathedral. He was one of the most outstanding church architects in Ireland of his time and he designed many churches and convents all over the country, including St Patrick's Cathedral, Armagh, St Macartan's Cathedral, Monaghan and the Cathedral of the Assumption, Thurles.

The actual construction work took twenty-two years to complete, at a cost of £40,000. It was not until 1873 that the building was brought to a stage where it could be dedicated and used for liturgical celebrations. The cathedral was dedicated by Bishop Francis Kelly on 4 May 1873.

In 1899 it was decided to add a spire to the tower, which was estimated to cost £15,000. The spire was completed on 19 June 1903, and on 27 June the eight-foot high granite cross was put in position by Fathers John Doherty and Lawrence Hegarty. The full complement of stained-glass windows was achieved in the Spring and Autumn of 1896 at a cost of £2,270. The ten bells of the cathedral first rang out on Christmas Eve, 1902.

St Eugene's was solemnly consecrated on 21 April 1936, the seventh cathedral in Ireland to be consecrated, and the event is celebrated annually on 21 April.

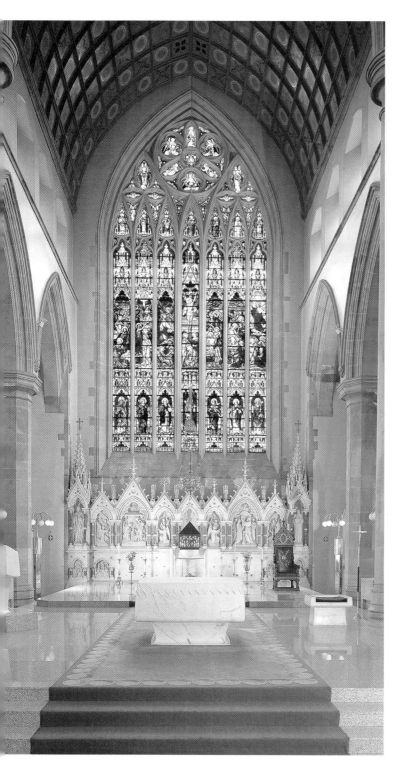

St Columba Window

This window was designed by Meyer of Munich (Germany) and installed in St Eugene's Cathedral during February 1895. It depicts St Columba, principal patron of the diocese, blessing Derry.

Diocese of Derry

HISTORY OF THE DIOCESE

THE DIOCESE of Derry includes the most northerly point of the island of Ireland, extends between Lough Swilly and the river Bann and includes most of the basin of the river Foyle. The ecclesiastical centre of the diocese nowadays is the city of Derry, founded originally by St Columba in 546 as a staging-post between Ireland and what would be his more important foundation at Iona in Scotland.

The area making up the present diocese was then a grid of *tuatha* or small kingdoms established by closely related kin groupings, for whom were founded the churches – many of them as episcopal centres – of Ardstraw (by St Eoghan or Eugene), Carndonagh (associated with St MacCairthenn), Coleraine (by St Cairbre, St Eugene's friend), Fahan (founded by St Mura), Maghera (by St Lurach), and the churches of St Finlugh and St Neachtan in the Roe Valley. Many of the churches of the diocese are so ancient that they were later claimed with some verisimilitude to have been founded by St Patrick himself.

With the passage of time the stronger of these kingdoms began to absorb the weaker, until eventually the whole area was ruled by one kin group, *Cineál Eoghain* (the descendants of Eoghan, son of high king Niall Naoighiallach – of the Nine Hostages +453). This process, supported by increased continental travel and contemporary developments in Scotland, coincided with the movement to reform the Church, associated with St Malachy of Armagh in the twelfth century. One of the most crucial aspects of this programme, influenced by Rome, was the establishment of territorial bishops. In the north-west, this diocese was to be based at Ardstraw in what is now Co Tyrone but, because it suited the secular power better, the diocese was in fact centred on Ráth Luraigh, now Maghera.

By this time Derry had become the centre of the religious order founded by St Columba. Part of the settlement of the Twelfth Century Reform seems to have been that the order conceded monastic primacy to Armagh. The Abbot of Derry, St Gelasius, became Archbishop of Armagh in succession to St Malachy, and his successor in turn, St Conor Mac Con Choille, had family associations with the abbey, which he perhaps influenced to accept the rule of the Canons Regular of Arrouaise. In any case Derry lost its Columban order, and in the thirteenth century became the seat of the bishop of the diocese in an area co-extensive with the then Mac Lochlainn kingdom of northern Cineál Eoghain.

Like the rest of Western Europe, Derry had its quota of 'Rome-runners' seeking ecclesiastical preferment, although they went first to Avignon. With the Norman invasion and the rise of English power, candidates for the episcopacy had to get permission from the medieval English king. This ceased to be a problem when English power broke with Rome. With the Plantation of Ulster (which dispossessed all native leadership), the wars of the seventeenth century and the Penal Laws, the diocese entered its own 'dark ages'. Catholics were tenants on their ancestors' lands and were not allowed any recognised place of worship. Being Catholic was not illegal but the English Government made it a test of loyalty, which it chose to constrain or persecute if it felt vulnerable. Catholics had to live outside town walls. The atmosphere in Derry was especially unsympathetic. Priests were discouraged, particularly those educated in continental seminaries, and bishops were forbidden. The diocese was without a bishop for 119 years after the martyrdom of Réamon Ó Gallachair in 1601, a period when vicars-apostolic ran affairs. It is not clear where clergy at this time were educated – the seminaries were beyond reach of most.

SAINT EUGENE

Although now known as Eugene (from the Greek meaning 'well-born'), his proper name is Eoghan, meaning 'born under [the protection of] the yew tree'.

According to his *Vita*, Eoghan was one of a large number of young people, including also St Tiarnach of Clones, captured by pirates and borne off to Britain. There he became a student at Candida Casa (Whithorn in Galloway) founded by St Ninian.

Eoghan returned to Ireland to what was then the north of Leinster and founded a monastery at Cill na Manach in Cualann, now Kilnamanagh, near Tallaght, Dublin. He remained there, according to the *Vita*, for fifteen years and trained 'not a few bishops and very many priests', including his nephew Caoimhín, St Kevin of Glendalough.

His next foundation was in the kingdom of *Uí Fiachrach Ard Sratha* (Ardstraw), to whom no doubt he came as a missionary and perhaps as a voluntary exile for Christ. While there was a monastic house at Ardstraw, tradition is always clear that Eoghan was a bishop.

Ardstraw came to occupy an important place in Ulster's ecclesiastical life and the name of its founder retained its prominence when the founders of similar churches were forgotten.

SAINT COLUMBA 521-597

Columba, secondary Patron of Ireland and of the Diocese of Derry, was born at Gartan on 7 December 521. Usually designated in Irish Colum Cille ('dove of the church'), he was given his early education by Cruithnechan, a priest who lived near Kilmacrenan. He became one of the pupils of Finnian of Clonard and was himself called to the priesthood. He also studied with Mobhi of Glasnevin. It was from Glasnevin that he returned north in 546 to found the monastery of Derry. He is credited, too, with establishing another major Irish foundation at Durrow.

In 563 Columba and twelve companions sailed from Derry via Moville to Iona to establish a base for the conversion of the heathen part of Scotland. Iona is a small island south-west of the larger Mull, about eighty miles north of Co Antrim. In Columba's time it lay within the Irish territory of Dál Riata, which was divided by the

North Channel. Using Iona as a base, Columba set up other foundations with the support not only of the Dál Riata but also of Pictish chieftains with whom he established good relations. Some authorities suggest that he founded thirty establishments in the Hebrides and along the west coast of Scotland, including monasteries on Hinba, Tiree and Skye.

Because of Columba's position and temperament he was a major figure in the political life of Dál Riata. He certainly played kingmaker in 574 on the death of the king of Dál Riata.

By the time the saint died in his seventy-seventh year, on Sunday, 9 June 597, his work of preaching Christ to the Picts was well in hand. The monastery at Iona had become the supreme Christian centre in Scotland. Columba's disciples, too, were to play an important part in the evangelising of Britain through the foundations in Lindisfarne and Whitby.

In the Diocese of Derry, Columba is remembered with particular affection in Derry city. There are modern church dedications to him in the parishes of Long Tower, Waterside, Ballinascreen, Moville, Iskaheen and Doneyloop. St Columb's College, Derry, and St Colm's High School, Draperstown, bear his name, as do thirteen primary schools throughout the diocese. St Columb's Hall in Derry and St Colm's Hall in Draperstown are dedicated to the saint. Adomnán, his biographer, is revered in Errigal (Garvagh), and Cruithnechan, his foster-father, is remembered in the parish of Desertmartin.

PLACE OF PILGRIMAGE

St Columba's Church, Long Tower

Tradition places Columba's monastery of Daire Cailcig in the spot where St Columba's church now stands. On this hill is the site of the 'Dubh Regles', the Black Church of Columba, or Teampall Mór as it became known when rebuilt in 1164. This church gave its name to the present city parish of Templemore. It was used by the early English settlers for their worship before St Columb's Cathedral was built. Later it fell into disuse and was used to store gunpowder. An explosion in 1568 reduced it to rubble and the stones are built into the city walls.

The round tower that gave the Long Tower its name survived to the early 1600s but no trace remains.

Two items link the Long Tower church with the days of Columba. St Columb's Stone, now built into the Calvary at the side of the church, has two deep depressions that local tradition ascribes to the print of the saint's knees as he prayed. St Columb's Well, down the hill from the church, is venerated as a holy well and on 9 June each year the water is drawn from the well and blessed to invoke the protection of the saint.

The present church building dates from 1783 and was sited beside the hawthorn tree where Mass was said in the absence of a place of worship. Since then the Long Tower church has been enlarged and decorated with many fine artworks – including a series of stained-glass windows depicting scenes from the life of St Columba. The church remains a focus for Columban devotion in the city.

Diocese of
Down and Connor

Down and Connor

Most Rev Patrick Walsh DD

Bishop Walsh was born in 1931 in Cobh, Co Cork, but his family then moved to Belfast.

He was educated at St Mary's Christian Brothers' Grammar School, Belfast, before attending Queen's University, Belfast, from 1948 to 1952, where he took a BA Degree in Mathematics. From there he went to the Pontifical Lateran University, Rome for four years, where he obtained a Licentiate in Theology. This was followed by two years in Christ's College, Cambridge, where he obtained an MA in Mathematics, and he was subsequently conferred with an MA from Queen's University.

At the completion of his studies in Rome he was ordained in St John Lateran Basilica in Rome on 25 February 1956.

In 1958 he was appointed to the staff of St MacNissi's College, Garron Tower, and remained there until 1964, when he was appointed Chaplain to the Catholic students attending Queen's University.

In 1970 he was appointed President of Malachy's College, Belfast.

In 1983 he was ordained Auxiliary Bishop for the Diocese of Down and Connor. In 1991 he was appointed Bishop of Down and Connor.

He is a trustee of Trócaire, a member of the Finance and General Purposes Committee of the Irish Episcopal Conference, Chairman of the Commission for Clergy, Seminaries, Vocations, a member of the Joint Bio-Ethics Committee of the Episcopal Conference of England and Wales, Scotland and Ireland, and a member of the Irish Bishops' Committee for Bioethics.

He is a member of the Council for Catholic Maintained Schools and Chairman of the Board of Governors of St Mary's University and the four Diocesan Colleges. He is also Chairman of the Trustees of the Mater Hospital.

St Peter's Cathedral, Belfast

Several bishops in Ireland began the building of cathedrals in their dioceses the 1830s and 40s. They usually chose the largest and most central town as the site of their episcopal administration, and their cathedrals were generally large and more ornate than the churches that were then being built in other towns.

Belfast had been chosen by Bishop William Crolly in 1825 as the seat of episcopal governance for Down and Connor. Ten years later he was transferred to Armagh before he could make any arrangements to build a cathedral. third church was required for the growing Catholic population, and Bishop Crolly successor, Bishop Cornelius Denvir, gave some thought to making the new church, St Malachy's, which was blessed in 1844, his cathedral. But paucity of resources had forced him to reduce the size of his plan, and the project of erecting a cathedral was abandoned.

With the big increase in the Catholic population in the 1850s, another church was needed in Belfast. A site was

'Mary, Mother of Comfort, Mother of Consolation', St Patrick's Church, Donegall Street, Belfast

This sculpture and tableaux by Chris Ryan of Dublin was specially commissioned as a tribute to the women, especially the mothers, of St Patrick's parish, Belfast, many of whom had suffered so greatly during the years of conflict.

Our Lady is shown presenting her Son to the world and inviting us to come to him – 'the Word made flesh, the Saviour of the world'.

The child is shown wearing two garments, symbolising the two natures of Christ, the human and the divine. He also wears a stole, an indication that he has come to serve and redeem the world. Our Lady is seated, pointing towards her Son with outstretched arms, reflecting Jesus' own words in the Gospel: 'Come to me all you who labour and are heavily burdened and I will refresh you' (Mt 11:28).

The third figure represents a mother approaching Our Lady for comfort and consolation, and being led by her towards her Son. The woman prays openly and with confidence and dignity.

...quired in 1858, and the foundation ...one of the church, dedicated to St ...eter, was laid in 1860. It was designed ... Jeremiah Ryan McAuley, a Belfast ...chitect, who, two years previously, had ...ecome a priest. Built in the Gothic ...yle, it cost £16,000. Among the many ...shops who attended the opening ...remony in 1866 was Cardinal Cullen, ...ho had received the red hat a short ...me previously, and the preacher on the ...casion was the Bishop of Birmingham, ...illiam Ullathorne. Since then, many ...terations have been made to St Peter's. ...n organ was installed at a cost of £1,400 ...1883, together with a carillon of bells ...sting £1,500, and the spires were ...mpleted in 1885 at a cost of £5,000.

...Peter's and St Patrick's churches were ...th used as pro-cathedrals by the ...shops of Down and Connor since the ...60s. In 1982 Bishop Cahal Daly was ...ansferred to Down and Connor from ...dagh and Clonmacnois. Shortly after ...s installation, he undertook a ...furbishment of the church, and its ...atus was raised to that of a cathedral in ...86. Further refurbishment is planned ...that St Peter's Cathedral will be an ...ornment in the regeneration currently ...king place in inner Belfast.

Diocese of
Down & Connor

HISTORY OF THE DIOCESE

ST PATRICK does not provide many geographical details in his *Confession* about his sojourn in Ireland. A later tradition associated his work as a slave with Slemish in Co Antrim, his return as a missionary with Saul in Co Down and his burial place with Downpatrick. Modern scholars, however, reject many of these traditions, which date from at least two centuries after his death.

In the course of his evangelisation of Ireland, Patrick ordained bishops to minister to local communities that had become Christian. Among those bishops was Mac Nissi, whom the saint had baptised, and who founded the church of Connor. But by the sixth century, when Christianity had been well established, the monastic system, in which the bishop was a member of the community, was becoming the dominant form of ecclesiastical life. About 555 St Comgall founded a monastery at Bangor, which was destined to become one of the most famous in the whole country. From it went forth to the Continent Columban, Gall and their companions, who in turn founded monasteries in France, Switzerland and Italy, which were to become influential centres for the conversion or re-conversion of many peoples. Other monasteries founded in the early centuries of Christianity in Down and Connor include those at Moville, Nendrum, Inch, Drumbo, Antrim and Comber. Some of these later adopted the Benedictine or Augustinian Rule.

The Norsemen cast greedy eyes on Irish monasteries, especially those near the coast, which could be easily attacked and plundered for silver and gold vessels. Bangor fell victim to one such raid in 823, when many monks were killed and the shrine of St Comgall was destroyed. The loss of life and damage to buildings helped weaken the discipline and commitment of the monks. When St Malachy, the great reformer, became Abbot of Bangor in 1123, he found much of the abbey in ruins and the Rule being poorly observed. He set about the restoration of the monastery and of

monastic discipline but was soon called to the bishopric of Down and Connor.

In 1111 at the Synod of Rathbreasail Ireland was at last given the diocesan territorial system that had been common in the Western Church. Among the dioceses created were Connor for the Kingdom of Dalriada and Down for that of the Uladh. Though separate, these dioceses were united under St Malachy in 1124. He continued to reside at Bangor and pursue his reforms, but was driven out from the monastery and forced to take refuge at Lismore in Munster. In 1129 he was appointed Archbishop of Armagh but because of local opposition was not able to take control of the see until five years later. In 1137 he resigned and returned to the Diocese of Down, which was again separate from Connor. Invited by his fellow bishops to travel to Rome to obtain the *pallia* for the archbishops of Armagh and Cashel, Malachy set off in 1139 and visited St Bernard at Clairvaux. Though unsuccessful in his quest, he was appointed papal legate for Ireland. He left some monks at Clairvaux to be trained in the Cistercian way of life, and they and French colleagues established the first Cistercian monastery at Mellifont in 1142. A second journey to Rome in 1148 to seek the *pallia* was cut short by his death on 2 November in the arms of St Bernard. The great Cistercian abbot later wrote Malachy's life, which ensured that his fame spread widely on the Continent, and he was cannonised in 1190.

In 1177 the Anglo-Norman adventurer John de Courcy carved out the Lordship of Ulster for himself and set up his base at Dunlethglaisse, which he renamed Downpatrick. He took a keen interest in ecclesiastical affairs and brought Anglo-Norman Benedictine monks to the cathedral at Downpatrick. His wife founded the Cistercian Monastery at Greyabbey in the Ards, and he brought other orders, such as the Premonstratensian and the Augustinian Canons to his territories.

In 1192 the Diocese of Dromore was cut off from Down to make provision for the native Irish, as the part that retained the name Down was by then regarded as

Anglo-Norman. The Diocese of Down and Connor continued to be administered separately until the fifteenth century. In 1439 Pope Eugene IV decided that the two sees should be united on the death of John Sely, the Bishop of Down. And though Sely was deprived of office three years later for misbehaviour, the Archbishop of Armagh resisted the union of the two dioceses for several years, and it did not take place until 1453.

In the 1220s the newly founded mendicant orders, the Dominicans and Franciscans, established houses in the diocese. By the sixteenth century the third order of Franciscans had numerous friaries.

Robert Blyth, an English Benedictine was Bishop of Down and Connor when Henry VIII demanded recognition as supreme head of the Church. Blyth surrendered in 1539 and received a substantial pension. The Pope then deprived him of office and appointed in his place Eugene Magennis. Magennis also accepted the royal supremacy but later retracted his submission and was able to retain his see under Mary Tudor. The Franciscan pluralist, Miler Mc Grath, who succeeded in 1565 and accepted the royal supremacy in 1567, was deposed by Pope Gregory XIII in 1580, but had already been appointed Archbishop of Cashel by Queen Elizabeth. Two years later the Donegal Franciscan, Conor O'Devany, became bishop, and after a lengthy episcopate of nearly thirty years was cruelly martyred in Dublin in 1612. (In 1992 he was one of the seventeen Irish martyrs beatified by Pope John Paul II.)

During the upheavals of the seventeenth century and the harsh penal legislation of the early eighteenth century, the diocese was left vacant for long periods. After the death of Bishop Daniel Mackey in 1673 no appointment was made until Terence O'Donnelly became vicar apostolic in 1711. When O'Donnelly's successor, James O'Sheil, died in 1724, the see remained vacant until 1727. After the death of Bishop John Armstrong in 1739 all subsequent vacancies never lasted much more than a year, and often much less.

In 1825 William Crolly, who had been parish priest of Belfast for thirteen years, became bishop. Several of his predecessors had lived in or near Downpatrick but he chose to remain in the growing town, which he rightly foresaw would become the largest in the diocese. Not only was Belfast geographically more central and convenient but its Catholic population soon dwarfed that of Downpatrick and of all other parishes in the diocese. By 1900 Catholics numbered 85,000 and represented just under a quarter of the city's population. The number of priests serving in it had greatly increased and religious orders of men and women had been brought in to care for the spiritual, educational and social needs of the people.

The continued increase in the number of Catholics in and around Belfast accounts for the position Down and Connor holds as the second largest diocese in Ireland, with population of approximately 300,000.

PLACE OF PILGRIMAGE

St Patrick's Shrine, Saul

St Patrick's *Confession* provides very little geographical or chronological detail about his life, and the little that it does provide has been the subject of much controversy. Many of the gaps in his life-story were later filled by Tirechán and Muirchu, who wrote in the second half of the seventh century, but since they had a 'political' purpose in composing their 'biographies', namely to further the aims of the monastic community of Armagh and of the Uí Néill dynasty to a greater control over other monastic foundations and kingdoms, and were writing more than two hundred years after the events they describe, scholars do not generally accept the additional information they supply about the national patron.

According to Muirchu, St Patrick, in response to a vision and voices begging him to come back to Ireland, set sail again for the country from which he had escaped, and after an unsuccessful attempt to embark in Co Wicklow, he landed near Saul in Co Down. The local chieftain, Dichu, who was at first hostile to the stranger but was won over by his gentleness, became a Christian and gave his barn to the saint as a church. That barn, or Sabhall Padraic, gave its name to the district that was first blessed by

Patrick's missionary activity. Muirchu also maintained that the saint died at Saul after receiving the last rites from St Tassach, the Bishop of Raholp, and was buried in Dun Lethglaisse (later renamed Downpatrick), though Tirechán believed that he was buried at Saul.

These traditions associated with Saul inspired the establishment of a diocesan pilgrimage in Patrick's honour in that parish in 1932. As the whole country celebrated the fifteen hundredth anniversary of the beginning of Patrick's mission, Bishop Mageean of Down and Connor organised the first pilgrimage to the place that was proud to boast such intimate links with the national apostle. On 17 March 1932 Mass was celebrated in St Patrick's Church at Saul, and then the bishop gave Benediction to the vast crowds who had gathered outside. A procession was formed and some ten thousand people were said to have made their way up the hill, where the bishop blessed the site and the first sod for the St Patrick's Centenary Memorial. And the hill that had been known as Slieve Wellian was renamed Slieve Patrick.

A distinguished sculptor from London, Doyle Jones, was commissioned to carve a large statue of St Patrick to stand atop the hill. As a result of various delays the work was not completed until 1938. On 12 June of that year Cardinal Mac Rory, Archbishop of Armagh, in the presence of six of his suffragans and some twenty thousand people, solemnly blessed the giant forty-foot statue of the saint, and the altar and Calvary group that had been erected close by. The Bishop of Kilmore preached on the life and work of Patrick, and the ceremonies, which had begun with Mass in the morning, were completed with Benediction given by Bishop Mageean.

Since then the annual pilgrimage is held on the second or third Sunday of June each year and pilgrims from all over the diocese make their way in the afternoon to St Patrick's Shrine, where Mass is celebrated in the open air. The large attendances testify to the enduring popularity of Patrician devotion in Down and Connor.

Diocese of
Dromore

Most Rev John McAreavey DD, DCL

Bishop John McAreavey was appointed
Bishop of Dromore on 19 September
1999, to succeed Dr Francis Brooks, who
retired in June 1999. He was born at
Drumnagally, Banbridge, Co Down, in
1949. He received his primary education
in Ballyvarley School (near Banbridge)
and in the Abbey Christian Brothers'
School, Newry. He received his
secondary education in St Colman's
College, Newry.

In September 1966, he entered St
Patrick's College, Maynooth; he took a
degree in modern languages in 1969 and
his Bachelor in Divinity degree in 1972.
He was ordained a priest on 10 June 1973.
He returned to Maynooth after his
ordination and completed his Licentiate
in Theology in 1974. He then did postgraduate studies in Canon Law at the
Gregorian University in Rome and
obtained his Doctorate in Canon Law in
1978.

From 1978 to 1979 he was on the
teaching staff of St Colman's College,
Newry. In 1979 he was appointed to the
Armagh Regional Marriage Tribunal as
an assistant to the late Fr Hugh
Mulvenna. On the death of Fr Mulvenna
in 1983, he was appointed Head of the
Tribunal, a post that he held until 1991.

In 1988 he was appointed Professor of
Canon Law in the Pontifical University
at Maynooth. He has written and
lectured widely on Church law. Since
1998 he has been on the editorial board
of the *Irish Theological Quarterly*. He is a
member of the Canon Law Society of
Great Britain and Ireland and the Canon
Law Society of America. Since 1994 he
has been Secretary of the Greenhills
Ecumenical Conference Committee.

Bishop McAreavey has been involved in
the pastoral care of married couples, and
also of children with special needs and
their families. He is a member of the
Committee of Coláiste Bhríde, Rann
na Feirste.

**St Patrick and St Colman's Cathedral,
Newry**

Newry cathedral was founded in 1825, a
the centre of a growing and prosperous
town. It symbolised, in many ways, the
increasing confidence of the local Catho
population of the day, especially the
newly emerging Catholic middle class.

The cathedral was designed by Thomas
J. Duff, a prominent architect in the
northern part of Ireland at the turn of
the century. The building was dedicate
in May 1829 by the then Irish Primate,
Dr Curtis. It was believed to be the first
major dedication ceremony in Ireland
following the granting of Catholic
Emancipation.

Originally, the cathedral was sparsely
furnished, and it received its first
significant interior decoration in 1851. T
building was developed considerably
between 1888 and 1891. During these
years, its two transepts were added and a
handsome bell-tower erected. From 190
to 1909, Bishop Henry O'Neill oversaw
further major phase of building. The
main body of the church was extended i
length by some forty feet and a new
sanctuary was added. Much of the
internal fabric of the cathedral, as we
know it today, belongs to this period.
Rich interior mosaic decoration was
undertaken, side chapels were constructe
and the cathedral's tubular organ was
installed. The cathedral was solemnly
consecrated in July 1925 – a century afte
its foundation! It enjoys the joint
patronage of Sts Patrick and Colman.

Interior renovation was necessary in the
wake of the Second Vatican Council.
This work of extending and refurbishin
the sanctuary area was undertaken by
Bishop Francis Gerard Brooks from 198
to 1990. It included the construction of
the present marble altar, the rebuilding
of the reredos of the former high altar,
now in three parts, and the relocation o
the bishop's chair to the front of the
sanctuary. This work of renovation has
earned widespread praise in the field of
contemporary ecclesiastical architecture

Granite statue of **St Colman**, sculpted by Fr Henry Flanagan OP, 1991 (Newry Cathedral)

St Colman, revered as patron of the diocese, is believed to have founded the see of Dromore about the year 514. His feastday is celebrated on 7 June.

The following words are from Fr Flanagan's homily on the occasion of the unveiling and blessing of the statue, 3 November 1991:

'The statue is left with a rough finish, the mark of the tools. The rough finish suits St Colman – those old Irish saints were tough, austere men and women....

I hope I have given him a kindly and strong face. He wears the Celtic tonsure – the Celtic monks shaved the front of their head as a sign of their dedication to God.

His dress might be called his walking out attire – the cloak, which was called the great mantle, made of rough, shaggy wool; his crozier, much shorter than the modern crozier; and his book of Gospels – very precious as it was written by hand, and he would have carried it in a satchel.

Why has he a small deer at his feet? One of the legends associated with St Colman tells of his kindness to a young hind which had lost her mother.... I like to

think of the story as showing the kind of man he was, kindly, down to earth, loving all of God's creatures, and, all the more so, his fellow men and women....

When you look on the statue, notice the pedestal which has just the name 'COLMÁN' on it. I trust that suggests how you should come with your prayers to St Colman – as to a brother or close friend whom you call by name, without any formality.'

Diocese of
Dromore

HISTORY OF THE DIOCESE

IN THE WAKE of St Patrick's successful mission, a monastic Church grew in Ireland in the fifth and sixth centuries. Monasteries were powerful centres of religious life and worship, but also of culture and learning. A monastery was established at Dromore, on the river Lagan, in the early sixth century, sometime between 497 and 513. Its founder is believed to be Colman, who had been a noted student in a monastic school at Nendrum. This school was located on Mahee Island in Strangford Lough, Mahee being a version of Mochay, the master of the school, who, it is claimed, had been a disciple of Patrick himself.

The location at Dromore was approximately midway between Downpatrick and Armagh, both closely associated with Patrick. Probably the first Abbot of Dromore, Colman is revered as patron of the modern diocese. He and his successors would have been powerful ecclesiastical figures in their locality, sometimes assuming, in practice, the role and responsibilities of a local bishop or, alternatively, living alongside a bishop who would have had relatively limited powers in the region.

Other prominent figures from the early Christian period include St Dallan, a blind poet and devotee of St Columba. He is believed to have been murdered in 598, and is credited with founding the church in Clonallon. St MacErc, a brother of Colman's teacher, Mochay, had charge of the church in Donaghmore in the fifth century. A fine tenth-century Celtic cross in the parish, although of a later age, is named after this saint. Bronach is the most prominent woman saint in the Christian tradition of this area. She is reputed to have been abbess of a religious community in the sixth century based in a valley between the present-day villages of Hilltown and Rostrevor. A bell, associated with her foundation, was recovered early in the last century and is currently displayed in the parish church of Kilbroney.

The establishment of a Diocese of Dromore, comparable to what we have today, was a consequence of the reordering of the Irish Church by Rome in the twelfth century. The area that formed the small diocese coincided with the medieval baronies or territories of Upper and Lower Iveagh, what we might term today south and west Co Down. It also included a portion of O'Neill land, that part of Co Armagh which lies east of the river Bann, and a tiny piece of south-west Co Antrim.

The diocese corresponded closely to the territory of the Magennis family of Iveagh, a Gaelic clan in the medieval period which came to prominence in the later twelfth century. Perhaps it was their growing influence that led to the constitution of the diocese around this time. Remember, too, the Norman entry to Ulster in the later twelfth century. They had been successful in what we would today call north and east Down but didn't really penetrate the south and west of the county. Another relevant factor may have been the apparent decline of the monastery at Dromore – its last recorded superior held office in 1159. A Cistercian monastery was established at Newry, dating from 1144. It was closely associated with the Magennis family and it continued prominently until the Reformation in the sixteenth century.

From the 1530s for almost three hundred years, Catholicism in Britain and Ireland suffered from the various political and religious upheavals that followed the Protestant Reformation. Monasteries and other religious centres were suppressed from 1536 and Catholic Church property was widely confiscated by the State. This came as a result of the Tudor King Henry VIII's decision to break away from communion with the Roman Catholic Church and the consequent attempt to establish a national, English Church, under the authority of the Crown.

In time, the supression of what was labelled 'Popery' throughout the Kingdom effectively meant the forcing underground of Catholic religious life and practice. Scattered throughout our diocese were Mass Rocks, where people secretly attended Mass. In this way they kept the Church alive in their locality, without public institutions or traditional structures. It is believed that there were many more of these Mass sites than we know of today, though some parishes have been able to locate them and have celebrated Mass there in recent years, e.g Clonduff, Upper Drumgooland, Magheradroll, Newry, Saval and St Mary's Clonallon. A chalice used for the celebration of Mass at one such site is still in the possession of the Bishop of Dromore.

By the mid 1700s it was clear in Dromore, as in the rest of the country, that Catholicism was far from extinguished. Catholicism began to reassert itself publicly and penal legislation was having, in practice, less and less force. The shifts in population that had occurred in the Reformation era were significant in Dromore as elsewhere. Plantations of English and Scottish settlers had ensured a Protestant majority within the area of the diocese. Roughly speaking, to this day, Catholics form a minority in the northern and central parts of the diocese, while they find themselves the majority Church in the more southerly parishes. It is not surprising, therefore, that Newry became the modern ecclesiastical seat of the diocese, being the key centre of Catholic population in south Down by this time.

Bishop Anthony O'Garvey presided over the diocese from 1747 to 1766. Still fearing to live openly in Newry, he resided with his family at Aughnagon, close to Mayobridge. During his time a number of Mass Houses were constructed and he is considered responsible for the constitution of his native parish of Clonallon and the neighbouring parish of Newry as the mensal or episcopal parishes within the diocese.

Dr Matthew Lennon (1780-1801) lived at Boat Street in Newry and he oversaw the construction of St Mary's Church in the town. It served as the Mother Church of the diocese for almost forty years. In 1823 the task of constructing the present cathedral in the entre of Newry began. It was opened in 829, the year of Catholic Emancipation. rom then on we see a rapid development f Catholic public life in Dromore. Between 1830 and 1860, twenty-five hurches were built, thirty-eight schools nd sixteen parochial houses. The iocesan college was firmly established n its present site at Violet Hill. Various eligious orders were introduced – Poor Clares in 1830, the Christian Brothers in 851 and the Sisters of Mercy in 1855.

The Great Irish Famine, 1845-49, led o widespread suffering and a very onsiderable growth in the rate of migration. That pattern of emigration ould be part of the economic life of the iocese, in some way, for the next entury, though not as severely felt as lsewhere. Dromore had approximately o,000 Catholics prior to 1845, by 1860 it ad around 60,000 and by 1910 around 5,000. Its current Catholic population approximately 65,000.

The later nineteenth century and the arly part of this century saw continued evelopment throughout the diocese ith the widespread building of national r primary schools and the construction f many of the parish churches in use oday. Following Partition, Dromore ound itself one of only two dioceses xclusively in the new Northern Ireland tate, though the bishop of the day, Dr dward Mulhern, had campaigned with ellow Catholics for an alternative rrangement. A Cathedral Chapter, or dvisory council of the bishop, non-xistent since the Reformation, was econstituted in 1918. The cathedral was ecognised with the title of Sts Patrick nd Colman in 1919, and a new bishop's ouse built at Violet Hill in 1932. The ociety of African Missions had stablished a house of studies at Dromantine in 1926.

Dr Eugene O'Doherty was bishop om 1944 to 1976. He attended the nonumental Second Vatican Council 962-65. In his period eighteen new chools were built as education was gnificantly reorganised by the Northern reland government. Two large churches ere opened – St Paul's, Lurgan (1966) nd St Brigid's, Newry (1970), reflecting ost-war urban growth in Dromore's vo largest parishes. A new parish of Moyraverty was founded in 1971 to cater or the 'new city' of Craigavon and its nvirons.

The episcopacy of Bishop Brooks 976-99) has coincided, largely, with the Northern troubles. These have brought pain and turmoil to many families and communities within the diocese, as they have done elsewhere. In terms of structural development, the period has seen the establishment of separate parishes within the traditional boundaries of Clonallon, centred on Warrenpoint, Burren and Mayobridge. Separate entities have also been recognised in Lurgan as St Peter's and St Paul's, Shankill. New churches have been built at Craigavon, Banbridge, Drumnavaddy, Ballela and Warrenpoint. The majority of existing churches have been renovated and the cathedral sanctuary has been significantly reordered.

PLACE OF PILGRIMAGE

Alt na tSagairt – Mass Rock in the parish of Clonduff

The ancient name for this spot before penal times was Alta Keltee or 'wooded hill'. The Carraig an Aifrinn or Mass Rock is situated high on the slopes of Alt na tSagairt mountain, which rises close to the Owenabwee or Yellow Water river. According to tradition, the local priest, Father Mac Eoghan (O'Hagan), used to celebrate Mass here.

A Cromwellian settler named Whitechurch, a long-standing enemy of the old faith, had erected a castle by the river Chann, and commanded a few troops of irregular horse with which he went priest-hunting. One particular Sunday morning the movement of people to Alt na tSagairt mountain was seen by one of the priest-hunters who had passed the night on Crotley mountain opposite and he quickly sped to Whitechurch's castle with the news.

Colonel Whitechurch and his men, along with a couple of his fierce bloodhounds, rode swiftly up the Kilbroney valley until they reached a road leading down into Newtown vale. There the colonel killed the priest, cutting off his head to take with him to gain the government reward. Many women, men and children were also killed. The bodies of the slain were scattered around the Mass Rock.

Some people who had escaped the massacre ventured out the next day and found the bodies of the slain, which they placed on a low-backed mountain-car. The remains of the priest and his flock were conveyed to Clonduff burial ground (dating back to the sixth century) where a great trench was dug and the victims interred in the ground of St Mocummog, where rest the ashes of countless generations of Magennisses, O'Neills and kindred clans. The grim memory is preserved and enshrined in the name it now bears, Glennacacinadh – the Glen of Kenning or mourning. The Mass Rock of Alt na tSagairt is now a hallowed spot.

Archdeacon Kearns, parish priest of Clonduff, organised the first pilgrimage on 15 August 1915. Bishop O'Neill of the Diocese of Dromore was present. Rosary and Benediction took place at the Benediction Rock. This event was to mark the transfer of the lands around this mountain to the people in 1914.

The next pilgrimage to the Mass Rock took place on 19 August 1917. Cardinal Logue and Bishop Mulhern were present. There was another pilgrimage on 18 August 1918, but owing to the disturbed political conditions in the country, Sunday 17 August 1919 saw the end of these celebrations.

The dedication of the new altar at the Alt na tSagairt Mass Rock took place on Sunday, 26 July 1931, at 4.00 pm. The Mass Rock in the townland of Leitrim – *Liath dhrom,* the grey ridge – was dedicated by Dr Brooks, bishop. The pilgrimage to the Mass Rock was again revived in 1979. At the dedication Mass, Bishop Brooks used a penal chalice of 1647 or 1657, a penal cross of 1722 and a wooden crozier used by bishops in the early 1800s.

Diocese of
Elphin

Most Rev Christopher Jones DD

Christopher Jones was born in Rathcroghan, Co Roscommon, on 3 March 1936.

Educated in Summerhill College, Sligo and St Patrick's College, Maynooth, he was ordained to the priesthood on 21 June 1962. In 1962/3 he taught part-time in St Muredach's College, Ballina, while studying for the Higher Diploma in Education at University College Galway. He returned to teach at Summerhill College, Sligo in 1965. In 1971 he spent over a year as Archivist at St Mary's, Sligo, while also serving as Chaplain of St Columba's Hospital, Sligo, and in 1972/3 he studied for a Social Science Diploma at University College Dublin. In 1973 he returned as first director of Sligo Social Services Centre, where he served until his appointment as Administrator of the cathedral parish in 1987. During that period he also served as spiritual director to the students of

Summerhill College, from 1973 to 1978, and afterwards as curate in Rosses Point, Sligo. For much of this time he also worked as diocesan vocations director. He served for many years as Chairperson of the National Council for Travelling People and is the advisor to the Minister for the Environment on matters relating to the accommodation of travelling people.

Canon Jones was appointed Bishop of Elphin on 24 May 1994.

Cathedral of the Immaculate Conception, Sligo

The 125-year-old cathedral church dominates the skyline of Sligo town. It was erected during the episcopate of Bishop Laurence Gillooly (1858-95), whose knowledge of ecclesiastical architecture is imprinted on every stone.

The foundation stone was laid on 6 October 1868. It was designed by a renowned English architect, George Goldie, and was modelled on Normano-Romano-Byzantine style. It was acclaimed by an eminent architect as a 'poem in stone'. It is 275 feet long, with transepts and nave, and can accommodate 4,000 people. A square tower incorporating the main entrance to the cathedral is surmounted by a four-sided pyramidal spire which reaches a height of 210 feet. The stained-glass windows and the original high altar are magnificent works of art.

Although the cathedral was open for public worship in 1874, it wasn't until 1882 that all construction work was completed. The cathedral was finally consecrated on 1 July 1897 and dedicated in honour of the Immaculate Conception of the Blessed Virgin Mary.

The cathedral has undergone extensive renovations on two occasions since it was erected, including the remodelling of the sanctuary to comply with liturgical norms in 1970.

Statue of St Molaise

The Statue of St Molaise is a unique and historic item in the archival material of the cathedral. It is a hand-carved wooden statue dating from the early stages of the foundation of the monastic island settlement of Inishmurray by Saint Molaise in about AD 500.

Inishmurray Island, which lies off the coast of Co Sligo, contains one of the most complete and visually exciting early Christian monastic settlements in Europe

Elphin

Diocese of Elphin

HISTORY OF THE DIOCESE

THE DIOCESE of Elphin has its origins in the local Church and can be traced back to the fifth century when St Patrick appointed St Asicus as first abbot-bishop of a monastic community in the town of Elphin, Co Roscommon. St Asicus was a skilled craftsman by profession, who used silver, copper and brass to execute many exquisite Christian works of art. He used his craftsmanship to give glory and praise to God, creating altars, chalices, book stands, crosses, etc. He established a school of art and learning in Elphin, inspiring the promotion of the arts and artistry in the Irish Church.

The monastic structure prevailed in Elphin until 1111, when the Synod of Rathbreasail constituted its first diocesan sees in Ireland. However, it wasn't until 1152 at the Synod of Kells that the present Diocese of Elphin was established.

The Diocese of Elphin is an amalgamation of the ancient sees of Roscommon, parts of Ardcarne, together with a portion of Killala and Tuam. So while the diocese dates from the twelfth century, the bishopric of Elphin is of much greater antiquity, dating back to the fifth century.

There is a well-documented account of the early Church of Elphin in the Tripartite *Life* of St Patrick, *the Book of Armagh* and the *Annals of Lough Cé.* The first cathedral church was built in Elphin about 1200, fifty years after the Synod of Kells, following the constitution of the diocesan boundaries. The earliest reference to a diocesan chapter is recorded in 1240. The spiritual welfare of the people of the diocese was well catered for by its diocesan clergy, as well as various religious houses strategically located throughout the diocese. There were as many as eighteen religious houses in the diocese, which survived to the sixteenth century. The cathedral church continued to be a place of worship until the late sixteenth century, when Catholic communities suffered much persecution and suppression during the Cromwellian Plantations and Penal Laws.

The diocese was deprived of a cathedral church for over three hundred years and only fully recovered religious freedom with the Act of Catholic Emancipation in 1829. In 1830 St Patrick's Church in Sligo town was designated the pro-cathedral of the diocese and it retained that status until the present cathedral was built in 1874. It was during that time that Bishop Laurence Gillooly (1858-95) transferred the episcopal seat of the diocese from Elphin to Sligo. However, the diocese is still officially known to this day as Elphin.

The present cathedral in Sligo has continued uninterrupted to be the place of worship for the diocese since the nineteenth century. A list of bishops who served the diocese since its foundation is on display at the entrance to the cathedral.

The seventy-seven original parishes of the diocese have been to a great extent amalgamated because of a shift in population and today they form thirty-eight parishes. Every parish has the remains of multi-period church ruins that served as places of worship over many centuries.

There are, however, a number of notable places and artefacts that are enshrined in the Christian heritage of our diocese, such as Inis Murray, off the coast of Sligo, Tobernalt in Sligo Town, Drumcliffe High Cross and monastic site, Trinity Island in Boyle, early ninth-century grave slabs at Fuerty in Co Roscommon, the Cross of Cong which was crafted in Roscommon, and several more significant places that point to a region steeped in religious practice and belief.

The Catholic population of the diocese now stands at 68,000 and is served by eighty-eight diocesan priests. St Asicus is the patron saint of the diocese and his feast on 27 April is celebrated each year at the old cathedral site in Elphin.

PLACE OF PILGRIMAGE

The 'Holy Well' at Tobernalt

A number of parishes in the diocese hold annual pilgrimages to places that have been traditionally recognised and associated with a particular patron day. While some of these places of pilgrimage declined in popularity in recent times, others continue to evoke much devotion and prayer, for example, Ogulla Well near Tulsk in Co Roscommon, Brideswell in the parish of Kiltoom and Cam, Tobar Mhuire in Elphin, Drum in Athlone, Trinity Island in Boyle, Inis Murray off the coast of Sligo and Tobernalt in Sligo. While all these places have their own distinctive Christian character and devotion, Tobernalt in Sligo is the most renowned.

Tobernalt is located at the south-west corner of Lough Gill in the parish area of Carraroe, Sligo. It is popularly known as the 'Holy Well'. It is a natural spring well that established itself in a primeval forest. It conserves an ancient past and embodies a rich Christian heritage. It was once the assembly site for the whole barony of Carbury and would have hosted the celebration of the festival of Lughnasa.

The advent of Christianity saw a fusion of Christian and Celtic traditions and brought a Christian dimension to the well at Tobernalt. The first Celtic Christians in the locality would have been baptised in its waters. There is a strong tradition that St Patrick evangelised there, but there is no evidence of the siting of an early Christian church adjoining this well.

Tobernalt continued to be a communal assembly place. The Lughnasa festival was christianised and came to be called Garland Sunday, which nowadays falls on the last Sunday in July. Each year Garland Sunday is celebrated as a patron or pattern day at Tobernalt, where pilgrims come in great numbers to participate in a special calendar of devotions.

During penal times, Tobernalt came a secluded haven for the ebration of Mass and people flocked re from the surrounding areas when ws spread by word of mouth that the est was expected.

After Catholic Emancipation, Catholics worshipped in newly built churches and chapels, but Tobernalt continued to draw pilgrims for private devotions. Major improvements to Tobernalt were carried out in the late

nineteenth and early twentieth centuries and the first Mass since penal times was celebrated on Garland Sunday 1921.

Tobernalt offers the pilgrim its own unique peace. It is a tranquil place of visitation, reflection and prayer.

Diocese of
Ferns

Most Rev Brendan Comiskey (SSCC) DD

Brendan Comiskey was born in Tasson, Clontibret, Co Monaghan on 13 August 1935. He received his primary education at Annyalla National School and Castleblayney Boys' School and his secondary education at St Macartan's College, Monaghan. In 1955, having completed a spiritual year at Sacred Hearts Novitiate, Cootehill, Co Cavan, he studied Philosophy at Wareham, Massachusetts and Theology at Jaffrey Centre, New Hampshire, USA. He was ordained to the priesthood in the Congregation of the Sacred Hearts at Tanagh, Co Monaghan on 25 June 1961. He pursued postgraduate studies in Theology as well as in the Classics at the Catholic University of America and the Lateran University in Rome.

From 1961 to 1964 he taught Latin and English and was Dean at Damien High School, La Verne, California, before moving to Rome, where he received a Licentiate in Theology. Subsequently he taught Moral Theology at the Washington, DC Theological Union and served as Chairman of the Moral Theology Department.

In 1969 he was elected Provincial of the Anglo-Irish province of the Congregation of the Sacred Hearts, and Secretary General of the Conference of Major Religious Superiors in 1974.

In November 1979 he was named Auxiliary Bishop of Dublin, with special pastoral responsibility for the south-eastern part of the diocese. In the same month he graduated with an MSc (Organisational Behaviour) from Trinity College, Dublin, the first Catholic bishop ever to graduate from there. On 20 January 1980 he was ordained Bishop at St Andrew's, Westland Row in Dublin.

On 20 May 1984 he succeeded the late Bishop Donal Herlihy as Bishop of Ferns.

A member of the National Episcopal Conference, Bishop Comiskey is

Chairman of the Bishops' Commission for Communications and President of the Catholic Communications Institute of Ireland. He is also a member of the Bishops' Commissions for Ecumenism and Education, and the Commission for Youth. He was a founding member of the Irish Churches' Council for Television and Radio Affairs (ICCTRA). He is Patron of the Wexford Festival Opera and was made a Freeman of Wexford Town in June 1990.

St Aidan's Cathedral

The foundation stone for St Aidan's Cathedral, Enniscorthy, was laid in 1843. The cathedral was designed by the architect Augustus Welby Northmore Pugin and is the largest church Pugin built in Ireland. The recent renovations of 1996 have restored to a great extent the original beautiful building as visualised by Pugin. The external stonework was executed by Irish stonemasons who were praised by Pugin. The restored stencilling of the interior gives some idea of what Pugin visualised for his churches.

Pugin, a Londoner, was as important an influence on the history of nineteenth-century English architecture as Frank Lloyd Wright was to be on American architecture. He was an extraordinarily gifted artist and designed ceramics, stained glass, wallpapers, textiles, memorial brasses, church plate, etc. His connection with the Diocese of Ferns came through the patronage of John, 16th Earl of Shrewsbury, Waterford and Wexford. Shrewsbury's wife was a native of Blackwater, Co Wexford. Her uncle, John Hyacinth Talbot, was the first Catholic MP for Co Wexford after Catholic Emancipation in 1829. A rich man through his marriage into the Redmond family, John Hyacinth Talbot introduced Pugin Wexford, where through the patronage of the Talbot and Redmond family connections, he was to gain most of his Irish commissions.

Pugin was to die through overwork at the age of forty in 1852, but he has left a unique diocesan heritage to Ferns in his churches. His son and son-in-law, E.W. Pugin and George Ashlin, were to continue the building of Gothic Revival churches and monuments in Ireland.

Includes almost all of County Wexford and part of County Wicklow

Diocese of Ferns

HISTORY OF THE DIOCESE

THE DIOCESE is celebrating its 1400th Anniversary in conjunction with the Jubilee. The diocese of FERNS (*Fearna*, the alder tree) was founded in 598 by St Maodhóg (Aidan), who received a grant of land at Ferns from Brandubh, king of Uí Cinsealaigh. Ferns had been the civil centre of the kingdom and now it became the religious centre also. During the episcopate of Maodhóg, some thirty churches and several monastic foundations were established. He died on 31 January 631. One of his successors, St Moling (+17 June 697), dedicated a holy well at Ferns in memory of the founder, which is now known as Maodhóg's Well.

One of the earliest monasteries in the diocese was that at Taghmon, near Wexford. It was founded by Fintan, also known as Munn. He was born in the north of Ireland of the O'Neill family. He became a monk at Iona and, after serving a few years in Scotland, came to Wexford. In 597 he founded the monastery that became known as Teach Munna, the house of Munn.

Christianity was known in this part of Ireland long before then. A monastery existed on the island (now reclaimed) called Beag-Éire (Little Ireland) in Inbhear Sláine, now Wexford Harbour. This was founded by St Ibar, whose death occurred in the year 500, according to ancient annals. Other early workers in the area were Sts Abban, Brendan and Senan.

During the ninth and tenth centuries, Ferns was attacked and despoiled on at least eight occasions by the Viking settlers before they became Christianised. The boundaries of the diocese were determined by the Synod of Rathbreasail in 1111.

In 1169 the first of the Normans came to Ireland via Bannow Bay in south Co Wexford. Strongbow, the Earl of Pembroke, in Wales, was invited to come over by the King of Leinster, Diarmaid MacMurchadha, who lived in Ferns. After this, Ireland was subject to the Norman king, who ruled England and part of France. The first king to have influence in Ireland was Henry II.

One of the results of the Norman invasion was the foundation of the Cistercian Abbeys at Dunbrody (around 1175) in the present parish of Horeswood and Tintern (1200) in Ballycullane.

In 1184 Ailbin Ó Maolmhuaidh, abbot of the Cistercian foundation of Baltinglass, succeeded to the see of Maodhóg. He attended the Fourth Lateran Council in 1216. He wrote to Rome requesting, on behalf of the Church in Ireland, the canonisation of Lorcán Ó Tuathail (Laurence O'Toole). His successor was an English courtier-cleric, John St John, nominated by King Henry III. After his death in 1223 the see was vacant for ten years, during which the king held on to the income.

Another noteworthy bishop was Patrick Barrett, a canon of Kells in Ossory, consecrated in Rome in 1400. He transferred the episcopal chair from Ferns to New Ross. He was Chancellor of Ireland from 1410 to 1413.

The last pre-Reformation bishop of the diocese was Alexander Devereux, abbot of Dunbrody Abbey at the time of its suppression by Henry VIII. He endeavoured to be loyal both to Rome and to the king. He died in 1566 and no Catholic bishop was appointed for fifteen years until Peter Power was appointed by the Holy See in 1582.

The previous year, 1581, six Wexford men were martyred for the faith – Matthew Lambert (a baker), Robert Meyler, Edward Cheevers, Patrick Cavanagh and two others whose names were not recorded. These were beatified on 27 October 1992. 5 July is the Feast of the Wexford Martyrs.

Bishop Nicholas French was consecrated in 1645, fled to the Continent in 1651 and lived in exile for twenty-seven years. He died as assistant bishop of Ghent in 1678. During this period, Daniel O'Breen, dean of the diocese, and James Ó Murchú, were martyred at Wexford on 14 April 1691.

Luke Wadding was appointed bishop in 1671 but was not consecrated until 1683. In a letter written that year, he stated that there were only twenty-one priests in the diocese. He died in 1691.

In 1798 there was an uprising against the British. Much of the fighting took place in Co Wexford. A priest of the diocese, Fr John Murphy, was one of the military leaders. He was eventually captured and executed. He has been immortalised in a very popular ballad, *Boolavogue*. Five other priests also died during the rising.

Very little is known about any missionary activity in the Diocese of Ferns during the Middle Ages. During the early nineteenth century a number of priests from the diocese worked abroad. Fr Denis Kelly spent seven years after his ordination in 1795 on the mission in Newfoundland. When he returned to the diocese he was appointed to Piercestown and later became known as 'the holy hermit of Kilmachree'. Two Franciscans from the diocese, Patrick Lambert and Thomas Scallan, were first and second Vicar Apostolic of Newfoundland in 1806 and 1816, respectively. Another Franciscan, Henry Hughes, a native of Wexford town, became Vicar Apostolic of Gibraltar in 1840. Fr James Dixon found himself 'a missionary by accident' when unjustly deported to Australia for alleged participation in the 1798 insurrection. He was appointed first Prefect Apostolic of Australia in 1803. He returned to the Ferns diocese in 1810.

Another young priest from the diocese, Thomas Hore, spent his early years in Richmond, Virginia, before returning home. In 1850 he led a group to the US and founded the parish of Wexford, Iowa. He is looked upon as founder of at least six other existing parishes in Allamakee County and several outside the county.

In 1811 a secondary school for boys was founded in Wexford town by the diocese. In 1819 this school moved to a site overlooking the town and became known as St Peter's College. After their course of studies there, many of the boys went on to study for the priesthood.

About eighty years after its inauguration, the Divinity School was opened. Prior to this, seminarians studied part of their course at St Peter's, but went to one of the other seminaries to complete their studies. The Ordination Class of 1901 was the first group of students to complete the entire programme of priestly training at St Peter's. Numbers increased over the years and in 1938 a new seminary building was completed. For the next thirty years the number of students in the seminary wing was close to a hundred. Numbers have declined since then and the seminary closed in 1998.

Seminary students came from all parts of Ireland as well as from the Diocese of Ferns. Most of the priests who worked in the diocese were trained in St Peter's. The other students were ordained mainly for English-speaking dioceses in many parts of the world, including Australia, New Zealand, South Africa, United States, and, of course, England, Scotland and Wales, as well as other dioceses in Ireland.

During the penal times, Catholics were not allowed to build churches (or hold public offices). After Catholic Emancipation in 1829, many churches were built – in fact, most of the existing churches were founded at this time. Some of these were designed by the famous architect, A. W. N. Pugin.

During the last century, Bishop Thomas Furlong founded many institutions in the diocese, including the Mission House in Enniscorthy, the Sisters of Perpetual Adoration and the St John of God Sisters in Wexford. He died in 1875.

Since the Second Vatican Council most of the existing churches were renovated under the episcopate of Most Rev Donal Herlihy (1963-83). Many new churches were also built.

The missionary activity of the diocese is continuing. In the early seventies some priests from the diocese made their way to South American countries, because they saw the great shortage of priests in that part of the world. As a result of their experiences, the diocese made a commitment in the seventies to supply priests to work in Brazil, in conjunction with the Kiltegan Fathers. Since then, many of the priests of the diocese have volunteered to spend a number of years there, to learn Portuguese and then serve in huge parishes. A few priests have also volunteered to work in The Gambia and South Africa.

PLACE OF PILGRIMAGE

Our Lady's Island Pilgrimage

This pilgrimage in honour of Our Blessed Lady is so old that the exact date of origin is unknown. It can definitely be traced to Norman times (twelfth century) because Rudolphe de Lamporte, who then owned the land, gave it to the Church and asked the Canons Regular of St Augustine to take charge of the island.

Rudolphe then went to fight in the Crusades, where he was killed. Before he left, he asked that prayers be said for the repose of his soul, and this should be remembered by modern pilgrims.

The pilgrimage continued until the seventeenth century, when, during the persecutions, the Augustinian church was destroyed and the priests murdered. Pilgrims are reminded that they are on holy ground which has been sanctified by the blood of the martyrs.

Pilgrims came to Our Lady's Island all through the penal times and continue to do so up to the present day. Every year hundreds come from all over Ireland to pray at the island.

The foundation stone for the present church was laid on 11 May 1863 and the church was opened on 15 August 1864. The annual procession of the Blessed Sacrament on 15 August was instituted in 1897 by Fr Whitty, then parish priest of the island.

Diocese of
Galway, Kilmacduagh and Kil

Most Rev James McLoughlin DD

James McLoughlin was born in Galway on 9 April 1929 at Cross Street, where his parents, the late Patrick McLoughlin and Winifred McLoughlin (née McDermott) ran a small wholesale grocery business. He received his primary education at the Patrician Brothers' school in Nuns' Island, and from there he went to St Mary's College, Galway.

He studied for the priesthood at Maynooth and was ordained on 20 June 1954. From 1954 he taught at St Mary's College, where he developed a keen interest in basketball and amateur dramatics. He was appointed Diocesan Secretary in September 1965. He served in this post under Bishop Michael Browne and Bishop Eamonn Casey until his appointment as parish priest of the cathedral in 1983.

His appointment as Bishop of Galway was announced by Pope John Paul II on Wednesday, 10 February 1993, and he was ordained bishop on Sunday, 28 March 1993.

Cathedral of Our Lady Assumed into Heaven and St Nicholas, Galway

In 1484, the Church of St Nicholas in Galway became a collegiate church, with a warden and vicars. However, with the Reformation, after 1570, the Catholic people of Galway lost the right to practise their religion publicly. Mass was celebrated in private houses until the rigour of persecution moderated and a parish chapel was built in Middle Street about 1750. The Diocese of Galway was established in 1831, and the parish chapel became its pro-cathedral. A fund for the building of a more fitting cathedral was inaugurated in 1876 and was built up by successive bishops. In 1883 the Diocese of Kilmacduagh was joined with Galway, and the Bishop of Galway was made Apostolic Administrator of Kilfenora.

In 1941, Galway County Council handed over Galway Jail to Bishop Michael Browne as a site for the proposed new cathedral. The jail was demolished, and in 1949 John J. Robinson of Dublin was appointed architect for the new cathedral. Planning continued until 1957, when Pope Pius XII approved the plans submitted to him by Dr Browne. Cardinal D'Alton, the Archbishop of Armagh, blessed the site and the foundation stone on 27 October 1957. The construction which began in February 1958, was undertaken by Messrs John Sisk Ltd of Dublin. The people of the diocese contributed to a weekly collection, and donations were received from home and abroad. The total cost, including furnishing, was almost one million pounds.

Pope Paul VI appointed Cardinal Richard Cushing, Archbishop of Boston, Pontifical Legate to dedicate the cathedral. The cathedral was dedicated on the Feast of the Assumption, 15 August 1965.

Galway

Rose Window above the Organ

The rose window is situated in the north gable of the cathedral. It has six large central panels or petals, with five smaller ones in between. In the large panels, beginning from the lower left, are shown the five Joyful Mysteries of the Rosary; on the sixth – the lowest panel – is the figure of the Immaculate Conception. The stained glass of the whole window was designed by George Cambell and executed by the Dublin Glass and Paint Company. The window was presented by the Most Rev Dr Browne.

Diocese of
Galway, KILMACDUAGH AND KILFENORA

HISTORY OF THE DIOCESE

THE PRESENT diocese of Galway was erected in 1831 and is, therefore, the youngest diocese in Ireland. Sometime in the late twelfth century a diocese known as Annaghdown came into existence in the area surrounding Galway city. In 1324 this diocese was united with Tuam, its metropolitan see. However, the Anglo-Norman families of the city ('the Tribes') refused to accept direct government from Tuam, and in 1484 the Archbishop of Tuam exempted them from his jurisdiction. Innocent VIII sanctioned this and made the city church of St Nicholas a collegiate church governed by a warden and eight vicars, who were 'presented and elected solely by the inhabitants of the town', i.e. the 'Tribal' families. This almost unique arrangement even survived penal times, so Galway city and its neighbouring parishes were administered by the vicars (canonically equivalent to parish priests) and a warden, who, though not a bishop, had all the powers of jurisdiction of a bishop.

In the eighteenth century there were continuous disputes between the archbishops of Tuam and the wardens over the jurisdictional rights of the archbishops in the city. From the early nineteenth century, canvassing, disputes and semi-rioting became a regular feature of the election of each warden. In February 1828 the Irish bishops decided to recommend to Rome that the wardenship be ended and a normal diocesan structure be established. On 27 April 1831 the Bull *Sedium Episcopalium* was issued by Pope Gregory XVI, erecting Galway diocese. On 23 October of that year the first bishop, George Browne of Athlone, was consecrated.

The Diocese of Kilfenora and the Diocese of Kilmacduagh were both erected and had their territories defined by the Synod of Kells in 1152. However, in 1751 these two dioceses were united. Because Kilfenora was in the ecclesiastical province of Cashel and Kilmacduagh in the province of Tuam, the Bishop of

Kilmacduagh was made the Apostolic Administrator of Kilfenora, and it was decreed that the next person holding episcopal jurisdiction in Kilmacduagh-Kilfenora would be Bishop of Kilfenora and Apostolic Administrator of Kilmacduagh. This system of alternation continued down to the last bishop, Patrick Fallon, who resigned in 1866. In that year the Bishop of Galway, John MacEvilly, was made Administrator of Kilmacduagh and Kilfenora.

In 1883, however, the situation was changed. The formal canonical union of Galway and Kilmacduagh (both dioceses belonging to the province of Tuam) was created and at the same time the bishop of that union was made apostolic administrator in perpetuum of Kilfenora (in the province of Cashel). On the day that these arrangements were made, Galway received a new bishop, Thomas Carr, the first with the title Bishop of Galway and Kilmacduagh and Apostolic Administrator of Kilfenora.

In September 1886 Bishop Carr was appointed Archbishop of Melbourne in Australia. He was succeeded in Galway, on 26 May 1887, by the then Bishop of Achonry, Francis J. MacCormack. On his retirement in 1908, at the age of seventy-five, Bishop MacCormack was appointed a titular archbishop. He died in November 1909.

When the Diocese of Galway was erected in 1831 the four parishes of Galway city were being served by the Catholic church of St Nicholas (built c. 1816-20), known as 'the parish church'. This now became the pro-cathedral for the diocese. Because of the economic circumstances of the time, the question of building a cathedral did not arise until 1876 when a bequest of £500 was left for this purpose and a fund established by Bishop MacCormack.

In April 1909 the Bishop of Clonfert, Thomas O'Dea, was appointed as successor to Bishop MacCormack. A native of the parish of Carron in Kilfenora diocese, he had been vice-president of Maynooth before his appointment to Clonfert. He announced his intention of building the cathedral and had plans

drafted by William A. Scott. However, Galway did not have a diocesan college to provide secondary education for boys intending to become priests of the diocese, so he gave priority to the building of such a college. The 26 August 1912 saw the fruit of his efforts when the first students entered St Mary's College.

Bishop O'Dea died in April 1923 and his successor, Bishop Thomas O'Doherty who was also transferred from Clonfert, continued building up 'the Cathedral Fund'. Shortly before his untimely death in December 1936, at the age of fifty-nine, he planned to start work on the construction. By that time the fund had reached the sum of £108,000.

In October 1937 Michael Browne, a priest of the Diocese of Tuam and Professor of Moral Theology at Maynooth, was consecrated Bishop of Galway. He brought to realisation the aspirations of his predecessors with the dedication, on 15 August 1965, of the new Galway cathedral – dedicated to Our Lady Assumed into Heaven and St Nicholas. As a consequence of the opening of the cathedral, the boundaries of the city parishes were altered in 1971 and a parish assigned to each of the religious orders in the city.

During the thirty-nine years of his episcopacy, as well as building the cathedral, Bishop Browne saw to the planning and building of some sixty schools and thirty churches throughout the diocese. He organised the title deeds of all properties. His conviction of the necessity for all young people to have proper opportunities for education saw to the building of post-primary schools outside of Galway city and inspired his continued interest in university and third-level education. He also served as Chairman of the State Commission on Vocational Organisation.

In preparation for the Second Vatican Council, Bishop Browne was appointed in 1960 a member of the Preparatory Commission on Bishops and the Government of Dioceses, and during the Council he was elected one of the sixteen members of the Commission. After the Council, with Cardinal Conway

e represented the Irish hierarchy at the
irst and Second Synods of Bishops,
967 and 1972. As a token of honour he
as conferred with the Freedom of
alway City on 20 August 1973.

Bishop Browne retired in 1976 and
as succeeded by the then Bishop of
erry, Eamonn Casey. On arriving in
alway, Bishop Casey was faced with a
apidly expanding city and a need for
ew churches. It was a time when no
arish could hope to keep pace with
sing inflation in its collection of funds.
o combat this, Bishop Casey devised
ie Meitheal Scheme, which enables a
arish to build its church without having
o pay interest to banks on borrowed
oney. Bishop Casey also established the
alway Diocesan Youth Services and, in
onjunction with the local authorities, he
eorganised the Galway Social Services.

In 1979, during the Papal visit to
eland, Bishop Casey organised the
ope's meeting with the youth of Ireland
1 Galway. He resigned as Bishop of
alway on 6 May 1992 and was succeeded
1 1993 by Bishop James McLoughlin.

LACE OF PILGRIMAGE

ilmacduagh

he ancient monastic settlement of
ilmacduagh is situated near the Burren,
out six miles west of Gort town. It was
unded by St Colman MacDuagh, a
ephew of Colman, King of Connacht,
1 the sixth century. According to
adition, King Colman was very jealous
f his daughter-in-law, Rhina, and he
nt two men to drown her and her
nborn child in the Kiltartan river near
ort. By the grace of God, she did not
own, but came ashore at Corker,
here her child was born. The child,
amed Colman, was baptised at Corker
y an old monk and his mother
mained in the Corker area until
olman was ready for school. As the
oy's life was still in danger, she sent him
o be educated at Aranmore, where St
nda had his monastery and school.

When he came of age, he joined the
onastic order of St Enda, where he
orked and taught for many years. He
as actually instrumental in building a
urch on the island in Kilmurray, which
as named Teampuill Mhic Duach.

Though Colman worked and
reached for many years in Aranmore, he
d a deep yearning to live as a hermit,
d his thoughts often dwelt on his

home place and the solitude of the
Burren. Eventually, in the last decade of
the sixth century, he returned to the
Burren. As his uncle was still King of
Connacht, he went deep into the Burren,
with one companion, and lived there in a
cave in a deserted place. He constructed a
little oratory at the base of a tall cliff,
called Ceanaille, and remained there as a
hermit for a number of years, until his
cousin Guaire became King of Connacht.

Guaire became aware of Colman's
presence at Ceanaille and he invited him
to build a cathedral in his territory and
set up a monastic institution there, and
so undertake the episcopal change of the
king's territory. Legend has it that St
Colman left the choice of site for his
cathedral and monastery to God's
providence and chose the spot where his
girdle accidentally fell to the ground as
he rode through the Burren. This famous
girdle was kept by the families of the two
most powerful lords in the area, the
O'Shaughnessys and the Hynes, for
many centuries.

The cathedral erected by St Colman
was a single oblong church, but naturally
there were many alterations and additions
over the years. St Colman then erected a
monastery and it seems that a great
number of monks – it is said almost a
thousand at one time – gathered there to
share the monastic life. To accommodate
the big numbers, several smaller
dormitories and little churches were
erected over the years. All was peace and

tranquil until the Normans came.
Kilmacduagh did not escape the plunder,
but it was probably at this period that the
round tower was built, so that monks and
their followers might escape the slaughter.

The round tower is almost 112 feet
high, and because it was bedded on soft
earth with no deep foundation, it is a
leaning tower, some two to three feet out
of perpendicular. The other buildings
were considerably damaged during the
invasion, and though the cathedral was
partly restored, it was wrecked again at
the beginning of the thirteenth century
by William de Burgo, in revenge for his
defeat by Cathal O'Connor. However, it
was restored for the Canons Regular of
St Augustine in the middle of the
thirteenth century.

The visitor to Kilmacduagh today
can see the partly restored Cathedral of
St Colman, and, nearby, the Leaning
Tower. There are also a number of other
buildings. There is a Glebe House,
which was the abbott's residence, in
good repair. There is Hynes' Abbey,
restored to some degree by the Hynes
family. Next to Glebe House is the little
church of St John the Baptist. Near the
cathedral is the small O'Shaughnessy
Chapel, which was cared for by the
descendants of the O'Shaughnessy clan.
On the other side of the road that leads
from Gort to Kinvara, there is Our Lady's
Chapel. When St Colman resigned his
diocese, he retired to the little valley of
Oughtmana nearby, to live once more as
a hermit, until he died on 29 October 632.

There are holy wells connected with
St Colman in Corker, Gort and in
Cluanaille in the Burren, and the people
of both localities go on pilgrimages there
on the saint's feastday. Kilmacduagh is
still revered by the people of Ireland –
about three hundred a week visit during
the summer months.

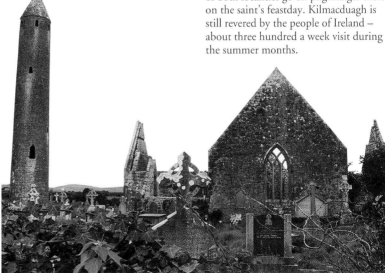

Diocese of
Kerry

Most Rev William Murphy DD

Born on 6 June 1936 at Annaghmore, Glenflesh, William Murphy was educated at Ratheen National School and St Brendan's College, Killarney. He studied for the priesthood at Maynooth and was ordained on 18 June 1961.

He taught for six years at St Colman's College, Newry, and then studied catechetics at Lumen Vitae, Brussels, and Fordham University, New York, where he was awarded an MA in Religious Education in 1969. He was Kerry Diocesan Adviser for Religious Education in primary schools for a year, before spending three years at the Gregorian University, Rome, where he was awarded a Doctorate in Divinity in 1973.

For the next five years he worked with the Primary Catechetical Commission preparing the *Children of God* series, the primary catechetical programme.

Fr Murphy taught theology in the Institute for Religious Education, Mount Oliver, Dundalk, for a year before returning to Kerry in 1979 as diocesan Director of Religious Education in post-primary schools and co-ordinator of Adult Religious Education in the diocese.

He was the first director of the John Paul II Pastoral Centre, Killarney. He became curate of Killarney parish in September 1987 and administrator in 1988. On the death of Bishop Diarmaid Ó Súilleabháin in August 1994, he was appointed administrator of the Diocese of Kerry, and bishop in June 1995. He was ordained bishop on 10 September 1995.

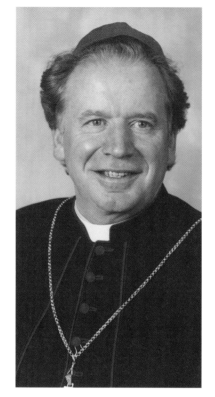

St Mary's Cathedral, Killarney

The Cathedral of Our Lady of the Assumption, better known as St Mary's, was designed by Augustus Welby Pugin. The main part of the cathedral was built between 1842 and 1855. Work was suspended between 1848 and 1853 because of the Famine and the building was used as a shelter for victims of the Famine.

Between 1908 and 1912 the nave and side aisles were extended and the spire, sacristy and mortuary chapel were added.

In 1972/3 the cathedral was extensively renovated. The intercom was reordered to meet the demands of the liturgical renewal that followed the Second Vatican Council.

Kerry

...rt in the Church of the Resurrection, Killarney (Built 1994)

...he Madonna and Child was carved ...om cedar wood by Imogen Stuart. The ...rtist said that when she looked at the ...ork after completing it, the words from ...he Hail Holy Queen came into her ...ind: 'Turn then, O most gracious ...dvocate, thine eyes of mercy towards ...s'. The Child appears in a risen posture, ...eflective of the title of the Church.

...What strikes people first when they enter ...he Church of the Resurrection is the ...apestry by Frances Biggs. It depicts ...ymbols of eternal life in God's Kingdom ...om the last book in the Bible, the ...pocalypse or Book of Revelation. The ...ymbols, from left to right, are: the tree ...f life, the Lamb, the white circle (the ...ternity of God, with no beginning or ...nd), the river of God's mercy, the dove

bringing the veil for the Bride of Christ, the new Jerusalem emerging in the background, the seven stars representing the seven churches to whom the message of the Apocalypse was addressed.

Diocese of
Kerry

HISTORY OF THE DIOCESE

WHEN THE bishops and clergy met at Rathbreasail in 1111 to reorganise the Church in Ireland, they established the Diocese of Ráith Maighe Deiscirt, which was co-extensive with the area of Iarmhumha. At the Synod of Kells in 1152, however, the corresponding diocese was called Ardfert, a title that was retained until modern times, when the diocese became known as Kerry. The great cathedral at Ardfert, built on the site of a previous church, became the seat of the local bishop. The first reference to the diocese in a papal document is in a letter of 1200 in which Pope Innocent III instructs the Arch-bishop of Armagh with the bishops of Kilmacduagh and Clonfert to install the legitimate bishop and to expel an intruder whose election was canonically null.

The twelfth and following centuries saw the introduction of several new religious orders into the diocese. The Cistercians founded an abbey at Odorney, the Canons Regular of St Augustine founded abbeys at Rattoo and Killaha, the Dominicans founded a priory in Tralee and the Franciscans established friaries at Ardfert, Muckross and Lislaughtin. These added a new dimension to the Church in the diocese. Due to the influence of the Normans, one notes the prominence of non-Gaelic names amongst many of the pre-Reformation bishops – de Valle, Ball, Fitzmaurice, Stack and Fitzgerald.

A change took place in the aftermath of the Reformation. All the abbeys and friaries were confiscated and a new type of priest and bishop appeared.

Following the Council of Trent (1545-63) Irish colleges were established on the Continent to train priests for the Irish mission. The first continental-trained bishop to be appointed to the Diocese of Ardfert was Rickard O'Connell, provided in 1641 and consecrated two years later. He was a native of Iveragh and was educated in France and in Spain. After his appointment as bishop he lived in Killarney, the first Bishop of

Ardfert to do so. In the 1640s he estab-lished a seminary in Tralee. Amongst those who taught there were Tadhg Moriarty OP, Conor McCarthy PP, Killeentierna, and Francis O'Sullivan OFM. These three priests were martyred by the Cromwellians and their causes for beatification are being examined in Rome. Unfortunately Rickard O'Connell's initiative failed. After his death in 1653 the diocese was ruled by vicars apostolic. In 1697 Denis Moriarty was proposed for promotion to the See of Ardfert. However, due to strong opposition from some clergy and gentry the appointment was delayed until 1720, by which time he was sixty-eight years old. He died in 1737.

In the early years of the eighteenth century the Penal Laws were enforced. In 1704 all Catholic clergy in the diocese had to register before a clerk of the peace, say where they were ordained and name the parishes under their care. Each parish was to have only one priest. Severe penalties were laid down to punish those who broke this law. This did not, however, deter other priests from ministering to the people. Although the Penal Laws may not have been enforced as rigorously after 1745, there were few enough churches in the diocese. Of those that did exist, most were just mudwalled buildings with thatched roofs. This situation gave rise to the custom of the 'Station Mass'. The lot of the clergy was no better. Bishop Nicholas Madgett built a house in Tralee, where he lived for £16-3-10. It wasn't until the nineteenth century that most of the churches were built with stone and roofed with slate.

The early years of the nineteenth century saw an improvement in the life of the Church in the diocese. Cornelius Egan, who had been in charge of an ecclesiastical seminary that his predecessor had established in Killarney about 1803, succeeded Bishop Sughrue in 1824. During Bishop Egan's episcopate he founded eight convents and built many schools. He was a great pastoral bishop, spending many hours hearing confessions. He witnessed the tragedy that hit the people of his diocese during

the Great Famine of 1845-49, when at least a fifth of its population died or emigrated. Six priests died from disease, caught while administering to the sick and dying. Others helped to organise food depots, while the nuns distributed what they could from their own kitchens. Bishop Egan made the, as yet, unfinished cathedral available to the destitute. During his latter years he suffered from ill health. In 1853 he petitioned Rome for a coadjutor. David Moriarty was appointed. On the death of Charles Sughrue in 1856, Moriarty automatically succeeded as Bishop of Kerry, as the diocese was now called. He was one of the great bishops of his day. He had been President of All Hallows College, Dublin and was responsible, to a large degree, for its rise as one of the foremost ecclesiastical colleges in the English-speaking world. As Bishop of Kerry, David Moriarty travelled the length and breadth of the diocese administering the sacraments and preaching to the people. He was a strong advocate of the national-school system of education and a firm believer in its role in catechising the children. David Moriarty built St Brendan's seminary, which would supply hundreds of students for the priesthood for the home and foreign missions. He invited the Franciscans and Dominicans to return to Kerry. He was a great believer in the benefits that flowed from parish missions. Under his guidance a major church-building programme was undertaken. He completed the work on the present cathedral, dedicated to Mary in 1855. The church in Kerry had found its feet. David Moriarty had laid the foundation on which his successors could build. They were Daniel McCarthy (1878-81), Andrew Higgins (1882-89), John Coffey (1889-1904), John Mangan (1904-17), Charles O'Sullivan (1918-27), Michael O'Brien (1927-52), Denis Moynihan (1952-69), Eamonn Casey (1969-76), Kevin McNamara (1976-84), Diarmaid Ó Súilleabháin (1985-94) and, currently, William Murphy (since 1995).

PLACE OF PILGRIMAGE

Skellig Michael

Sceilig Mhichíl or Skellig Michael is located some eight and a half miles off the coast of south Kerry. Its monastic remains have been declared a World Heritage Site by UNESCO; it ranks with the likes of the Pyramids, the Great Wall of China, Chartres, the Acropolis and the Taj Mahal as one of the most important heritage sites on this planet.

In terms of the Christian heritage of Kerry it is one of our most precious and inspiring places, remaining as it does in an 'in-between place' – between earth and heaven, between land and the great deep, between worldly concerns and those of the spirit. It is an extraordinary place, remote, often inaccessible, inspiring and always challenging.

In about AD 200, Daire Domhain, King of the World, is said to have paused a while off the Skelligs to gather his forces before the great battle with the Fianna at Ventry Strand, Cath Fionntrá. In the Irish Annals, Skellig is referred to from the fifth century as a place of retreat and refuge. The name Sceilig Mhichíl comes from the tradition that St Michael appeared here with all the Heavenly Host of Angels in order to help Patrick banish the serpents from Ireland. It ranks with Mont St Michel and St Michael's Mount in Cornwall as one of the great coastal Christian sites associated with the archangel Michael.

It is known simply as 'Skellig' or Scelig in the eighth- and ninth-century entries; it becomes known as Skellig Michael after the tenth century. The building of the medieval church may have been undertaken to celebrate the new dedication; this probably took place in the late tenth or early eleventh century.

Skellig Michael rises to 714 feet at its highest point. The monastic site at the north-eastern pinnacle of the island is at a height of 600 feet above sea-level.

The monastery developed between the sixth and eighth centuries. The monastic site contains six beehive cells, clochán, and two oratories, as well as a number of stone crosses and slabs, a number of graves and two wells. It also contains a later medieval church as mentioned. It has been estimated that no more than twelve monks and an abbot lived here at any one time, a number that has its own significance. The monks built a series of steps or stairways at three points, an extraordinary achievement in this place.

Higher still on the other peak of the island, at 700 feet above sea-level, is a hermitage that clings to the ledges of the rock. In the third century Christians from Egypt withdrew to the desert to live lives of prayer, fasting and meditation. This began as a withdrawal into solitude, but in the early fourth century groups of these ascetics began to live in common. In the province of Thessaly in Greece, in a place where bare rock was eroded into isolated columns, hermits established themselves from the fourteenth century

onwards on these columns. A network of hermitages and monasteries evolved, accessible only by ropes and nets. This group is called Meteora – 'suspended from the air'. The hermitage on Skellig Michael is at least five hundred years older and the monastery is older again.

We know little about the founding of the monastery. It is attributed to Fionán, whose cult is still strong in the south Kerry area. The earliest reference we have is found in the *Martyrology of Tallaght*, which was compiled towards the end of the eighth century. This refers in an entry for 28 April to the death of a monk of Skellig called Suibni. In the *Annals of Ulster* and *The Annals of Inisfallen* there is record of a Viking attack in 823 in which Etgal, the Abbot of Skellig, was carried off and left starve to death. Other Viking attacks are recorded at different times during the ninth century. The contact between Vikings and Skellig was not all one way or destructive, however. Legend has it that a hermit from Skellig baptised the famous Olav Trygvasson in 993; he was to become King of Norway and was the father of Olav II, who became the patron saint of Norway.

Life on the Skellig must have been difficult at the best of times. It has been suggested that the site was not inhabited in the winter, but we can't be sure about this. Access to the island must have presented a problem and the community could have been isolated for long stretches, even during the summer. They would have had fish, eggs and seabirds to sustain them, and the monastic garden they cultivated is a marvel in itself. Experiments have shown that they achieved a micro-climate in this sheltered and carefully cultivated place, which allowed vegetables to grow at twice the speed of mainland sites. A carefully engineered system for collecting and purifying water was also developed.

Despite its isolation, the monastic site is quite sophisticated and shows how this community managed to deal with the often hostile environment. It seems that living conditions along the Atlantic islands of Ireland became almost impossible due to changes in climate in the thirteenth century. Year-round occupancy of Skellig Michael became too difficult and the monks retreated to the mainland. Here, at the new Augustinian foundation at Ballinskelligs, the links with Skellig Michael were maintained. The island probably continued as a place of summer retreat and the community would certainly have been involved with the many pilgrims who came to the island. Skellig is listed as a penitential station for pilgrims undertaking penance in the early sixteenth century for example, and we have accounts from the eighteenth century of pilgrims coming from all over Ireland and from Europe at Easter to follow the Stations of the Cross and to kiss the stone slab near the hermitage on the southern pinnacle (this was a hazardous undertaking, and the slab has now disappeared, probably a victim of the extreme conditions of its location).

Even today, with mass tourism bringing many visitors to the Skellig, many of those who go carry the spirit of pilgrimage in them and find, as many before them found, that this place at the edge of the world is still one of the great pilgrimage places of Europe and the world.

Diocese of
Kildare and Leighlin

Most Rev Laurence Ryan DD

A native of the parish of St Mullins, Co Carlow, Bishop Ryan was born on 13 May 1931. He was ordained to the priesthood on 17 June 1956 for the Diocese of Kildare and Leighlin.

In 1958 he joined the teaching staff of St Patrick's College, Carlow and was President there from 1974 to 1980. He was Parish Priest of Naas from 1980 to 1985 and Vicar General of Kildare and Leighlin from 1975 to 1987. In 1976 he was appointed President of the National Conference of Priests of Ireland, a position he held until 1982. He served as Secretary of the Irish Theological Association from 1966 to 1971, and Chairman from 1974 to 1976. He was ordained Coadjutor Bishop of Kildare and Leighlin on 9 September 1984, and succeeded as Bishop of Kildare and Leighlin on 10 December 1987. He has been President of the Irish Commission for Justice and Peace since 1995 and Chairman of the Jubilee 2000 Committee since 1997.

Bishop Ryan has established structures for the promotion of collaborative ministry between bishop, priests, religious and laity at diocesan, deanery and parish levels.

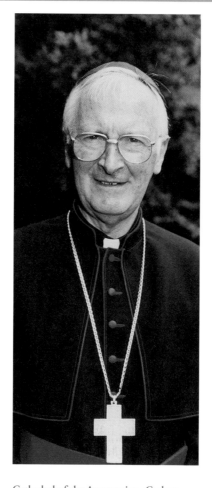

Cathedral of the Assumption, Carlow

The ancient cathedrals of the Dioceses of Kildare and Leighlin passed into Protestant usage in the period of the Reformation. Thus the cathedrals of Kildare and Old Leighlin stand on the sites of the ancient monasteries of St Brigid and St Laserian. Even before the Catholic Emancipation Act passed through the Westminster Parliament (1829), Bishop James Doyle OSA was working on the building of the Cathedral of the Assumption, Carlow. It is built on the site of and incorporates parts of the previous parish church of Carlow, which had been built in the 1780s by Dean Henry Staunton.

Carlow cathedral is not particularly large, having more the dimensions of a big parish church. The architectural work was begun by Joseph Lynch, but the final building is stamped with the design of Thomas Cobden, who replaced Lynch in 1829. Cobden gave the cathedral quite an elaborate exterior, with the obvious influence of the Bruges Town Hall tower. The cost of the building work was about £9,000. At its opening in November 1833, the interior decoration was incomplete. In fact, many elements were integrated over the following hundred years, sometimes adding to the mixture of styles.

The cathedral was consecrated on the occasion of its centenary, on 29 November 1933. A thorough reordering of the interior was completed in 1997, giving a very bright, welcoming, prayerful location for both diocesan and parish liturgical celebrations. The most notable elements are: the baptistry, the aumbry, the bishop's and president's chairs, and the Hogan statue of James Doyle, former Bishop of Kildare and Leighlin popularly known as JKL.

Kildare

& Leighlin

L Statue by John Hogan

1837 John Hogan won the
mmission for the memorial to James
oyle, Bishop of Kildare and Leighlin,
competition with ten other sculptors.
he work was finished in Rome in 1839.
was brought to Ireland and exhibited
the Royal Exchange in Dublin before
was placed in the cathedral.

eorge Petrie described the statue in the
ish *Penny Journal* of 1840: 'The subject
the last appeal of a Christian prelate to
aven for the regeneration of his
untry. Erin is represented resting on

one knee, her body bent and humbled,
yet in her majestic form retaining a
fullness of beauty and dignity in her
character, her turret crowned head
resting on one arm while the other, with
an expression of melancholy
abandonment, reclines on and strums
her ancient harp.'

Hogan was born in Tallow, Co
Waterford, in 1800 and is acknowledged
as one of the finest sculptors of the
nineteenth century. He died on 27
March 1858 and is buried in Glasnevin
cemetery.

Diocese of
Kildare & Leighlin

HISTORY OF THE DIOCESE

THE PRESENT double diocese of Kildare and Leighlin, with its fifty-six parishes, has a 'united' history since 1678.

KILDARE DIOCESE UP TO 1678

Kildare diocese owes its origin to the development from about the year 470 of a monastic complex at Kildare (Church of the Oak Tree) associated with the figure of St Brigid. Brigid worked closely with St Conleth, who is regarded as the first Bishop of Kildare. His consecration is dated about 490. The Four Masters record that he died on 3 May 519. After his time a monastery of men developed at Kildare. A succession of abbots of Kildare also functioned as bishops. The monastery was located in a circular enclosure. A Life of St Brigid written in the ninth century describes the great church in Kildare, 'a large high building with the decorated shrines of Brigid and Conleth at either side of the altar'. In 836 the Danes destroyed Kildare by fire and sword and carried away the rich shrines of the two saints.

Killeigh (Co Offaly) was another famous location in the Diocese of Kildare. St Senchall, supposedly St Patrick's first convert, established a monastery there. Later the monastery was known as the Priory of the Holy Cross of Canons Regular of St Augustine. Killeigh was plundered in 1537.

Finn O'Gorman, Abbot of Newry, became Bishop of Kildare in the twelfth century. He authored *The Book of Leinster* for Dermot MacMurrough, King of Leinster.

The Cistercians established an abbey in Monasterevan (Rosglas) in 1178. St Evan and St Abban were associated with an earlier Celtic monastery there from the sixth century. The Cistercian abbey was disbanded in 1539.

In 1223 Ralph de Bristol succeeded as bishop. He built a new stone cathedral at Kildare, which was mostly destroyed in 1641 during the rebellion.

The Dominican, Roche Mac-Geoghegan, became bishop in 1630. In the penal period, in common with most dioceses, Kildare could hardly support a bishop. Oliver Plunkett as Primate recommended that Rome amalgamate Kildare with the Diocese of Leighlin. In 1678 Pope Bl. Innocent XI gave Leighlin *in commendam* to Mark Forstall OSA, already Bishop of Kildare since 1676.

LEIGHLIN DIOCESE UP TO 1678

St Laserian (Molaise) was a grandson of Aidan, king of the Scots. He spent fourteen years in Rome and studied under St Gregory the Great, who ordained him a priest and sent him back to Ireland. He settled in the monastery at Leighlin (Co Carlow) founded by St Gobban. Laserian succeeded Gobban as abbot of the Leighlin monastery about 630. He undertook a trip to Rome in 633 to get a resolution of the controversy surrounding the date of Easter. Pope Honorius I consecrated him bishop and appointed him legate to Ireland. Laserian is credited with resolving the controversy in the southern half of Ireland. Leighlin may have had as many as 1500 monks at one stage. Laserian died in 639 and his feast as patron of the Diocese of Leighlin is on 18 April. The church of Laserian was destroyed by fire in 1060. The present stone cathedral (C of I) in Old Leighlin was commenced by Bishop Donatus in the years 1152-81.

St Fintan founded the famous monastery of Clonenagh (Co Laois) in 548. It continued as a place of learning until the eleventh century. St Mullins was the location of a significant monastic development and is named after its founder, Naomh Moling. Killeshin, Co Laois, has a beautifully preserved Romanesque doorway in the remains of its monastic church. Timahoe (Co Laois) has a completely preserved round tower.

From the twelfth century, new religious orders were established under the influence of the Normans. Leighlin diocese had three Cistercian foundations: Abbeyleix (1183), Baltinglass (1148) and Duiske Abbey (Graignamanagh, 1204). Also there were Carmelites in

Leighlinbridge and Franciscans in Carlow town for several centuries.

In the Reformation period Leighlin was governed by vicars general. A spanish Franciscan, Francis de Ribera, would seem never to have set foot in Leighlin after his appointment in 1587. The final Bishop of Leighlin was Edmund Dempsey OP (1642-61). His episcopate coincided with the Confederacy of Kilkenny and the Cromwellian campaign in Ireland. He died in exile in Gallicia.

THE 'UNITED' DIOCESES OF KILDARE AND LEIGHLIN AFTER 1678

The first bishop of both Kildare and Leighlin, Mark Forstal, died in exile in Cashel in 1681. After just three years of the new arrangement, the clergy of Leighlin petitioned to have Leighlin annexed to Ossory. The petition was unsuccessful.

Edward Murphy who served as bishop (1715-24) became Archbishop of Dublin (1724-29). James Gallagher, Bishop of Raphoe (1725-37), was transferred to Kildare and Leighlin (1737-51). His publication of *Sermons* went through several editions in Irish and English. Tradition holds that he conducted a type of small seminary in the Bog of Allen. James Keefe was bishop from 1752 to 1787. He resided mainly at Tullow, Co Carlow. After the passing of Luke Gardiner's Act of Relief of some Penal Laws regarding Catholic schools 1782, Bishop Keefe transferred to Carlow town to oversee the building of Carlow College for the education of both lay and ecclesiastical students.

Richard O'Reilly, PP Kilcock and coadjutor to Dr Keefe (1781-83), became coadjutor in Armagh and subsequently Archbishop of Armagh (1783-1818). The next bishop, Daniel Delany, had been Keefe's coadjutor since 1783. He oversaw Carlow College from its opening in 1793 appointing Dean Henry Staunton, PP of Carlow, to be the first President. Carlow College has had an illustrious history, preparing men for the professions in the Lay College up to 1892 and educating over 3,600 to serve in the priesthood.

During his episcopacy, Daniel Dela

founded two teaching orders, Brigidine
Sisters (1808) and Patrician Brothers (1809).
Their Mother Houses are in Tullow.
The Presentation Sisters came to Carlow
town in 1811, leading to the founding of
many convents in the whole diocese.

Peter Kenney SJ, who had studied in
Carlow in 1801-4, became in 1814 the
founder and first Rector of Clongowes
Wood College near Clane, Co Kildare.

After the short episcopacy of Michael
Corcoran came the most famous bishop
of the united dioceses of Kildare and
Leighlin. In 1819 James Doyle OSA, a
professor at Carlow College since 1813,
was consecrated bishop. He became well
known for his writings under the initials
KL (James Kildare & Leighlin). He
took on the political powers of his day
and was in close contact with Daniel
O'Connell in the fight for Catholic
emancipation. He completed the
building of Carlow cathedral in the years
1828-33. He died in 1834. In 1825 Dr
Doyle occupied Braganza House
(Carlow), which continued to be the
episcopal residence until 1969.

Catherine McAuley, founder of the
Sisters of Mercy, opened St Leo's
convent in Carlow in 1837. Schools were
opened in several parishes by teaching
sisters and brothers throughout the
nineteenth century. St Mary's College,
Knockbeg, absorbed the Carlow Lay
College in 1892 and is now a boarding
and day school for boys.

Several church buildings in the
diocese are from the second half of the
nineteenth century. About one third are
from the twentieth century. Most churches
built before 1965 have been reordered
according to the needs of the revised
liturgy. The newest church is that of the
Irish Martyrs in Ballycane, Naas (1997).

Three long episcopates dominate the
period 1856-1967: James Walshe (1856-88),
Patrick Foley (1896-1926) and Thomas
Keogh (1936-67). A Vincentian priest,
James Lynch, was bishop in succession to
Walshe (1888-96). His main contribution was in relation to the religious
congregations of the diocese. During the
episcopate of Matthew Cullen (1927-36),
the new Missionary Society of St Patrick
was established in the diocese at Kiltegan,
Co Wicklow.

To Bishop Patrick Lennon (1968-87)
fell the lot of implementing the changes
resulting from the Second Vatican
Council. He created several new parishes
and blessed many modern and renovated
churches.

Photo of St Mullins: Con Brogan, Dúchas. Image supplied by Archaeology Ireland.

The present bishop, Laurence Ryan,
whose episcopate began in December
1987, is a native of St Mullins, Co
Carlow.

PLACE OF PILGRIMAGE

St Mullins, Co Carlow

St Mullins is a village situated on the east
side of the river Barrow in south Carlow.
It is named after St Moling, who founded
a monastery there in the seventh century.
Surviving from the early period of that
monastic foundation is the *Book of
Mulling* (Moling) which dates probably
from the eighth century and is now in
the Library of Trinity College, Dublin.
This is a pocket manuscript in the Gaelic
script of the four Gospels in Latin.

The monastic settlement was
plundered by the Vikings in the early
ninth century. There are annalistic
references to the deaths of clerics who
held joint ecclesiastical offices in St
Mullins and Ferns and in St Mullins and
Glendalough in the tenth and eleventh
centuries. In 1150 St Mullins was granted
to the Augustinian abbey of Ferns.
Around the year 1300 it was granted to
the Cistercian abbey of Tintern, Co
Wexford. In 1323 the church at St Mullins
and relics of St Moling were burned.

A number of ruins remain: the
damaged head and upper part of the
shaft of a ninth-century granite High
Cross, a holy well, the base of a round
tower which dates from about 1100, the
ruins of a number of churches and
domestic buildings – the oldest of the
churches dating from about 1000.

St Mullins has been a place of
pilgrimage from at least the twelfth
century. The tradition of pilgrimage still
continues in the 'Pattern', which is held
each year on the Sunday before the feast
of St James, the patron of pilgrims (25
July) and which attracts large crowds
from neighbouring counties. The
pilgrimage element of the Pattern
consists of prayer at family graves in the
cemetery, drinking from the Blessed
Well, visiting the ruins and the
celebration of Mass at a Penal Day Altar
in the cemetery.

The feast of St Moling is celebrated
on 17 June by the people of the parish.
They gather for Mass on that date at the
site of another old church –
Templenaboe. This site owes its name to
the great achievement attributed to St
Moling in the Lives and other sources –
his success in having the Borrumean
tribute abolished. This was a yearly tax
of cattle which the men of Leinster had
to pay to the King of Tara.

Diocese of
Killala

Most Rev Thomas A. Finnegan DD, DCL

Born on 26 August 1925 of Patrick Finnegan and Margaret Connaughton, Cloonfellive, Castlerea, Co Roscommon, Thomas Finnegan was educated at Runnamoat National School, Roscommon CBS primary school and Summerhill College, Sligo. He studied for the priesthood at St Patrick's College, Maynooth, and was ordained for the Diocese of Elphin on 17 June 1951.

After ordination he taught in the Catholic University School, Dublin, and obtained the Higher Diploma in Education at UCD. Afterwards he obtained a Doctorate in Canon Law at Maynooth, then returned to Sligo where he served as Diocesan Secretary and Chaplain to St Angela's College until 1960, when he was appointed to Maynooth as Dean. He was President of Summerhill College, Sligo (1966-1979) when he was appointed Director of the Galway Regional Marriage Tribunal. In 1982 he became Parish Priest of Roscommon, from which he was appointed Bishop of Killala in 1987.

As Bishop of Killala he has, with the collaboration of priests, religious and parishioners, promoted the establishment of parish pastoral councils and a diocesan pastoral council. In 1991 the Killala Diocesan Mission to Brazil was inaugurated and a new Pastoral Centre was opened in Ballina. In 1995 Bishop Finnegan opened Holy Hill Hermitage at Skreen, Co Sligo, to which he invited the founder and members of the Spiritual Life Institute. In 1998 he opened the Newman Institute Ireland in Ballina, which has been planned as phase one of a Catholic university.

As a member of the Bishops' Conference Bishop Finnegan has served on the Bishops' Commission for Emigrants, the Bishops' Commission for Education, and the Bishops' Commission for Catechetics, of which he is the current chairperson. He is also a member of the Liaison Committee of the Bishops' Conferences of Ireland, England and

Wales, and Scotland. He has served on the Standing Committee of the Irish Bishops' Conference and on the Maynooth College Executive Council. He was a founder member of the Western Bishops' Initiative 'Developing the West Together' and is currently a member of the Council for the West, set up by the Western Bishops in 1994.

Bishop Finnegan's writings include: *Sligo: Sinbad's Yellow Shore* (Dolmen Press), *Branch of the Vine* (The Furrow Trust), and articles for journals including *The Furrow, Studies, An Sagart* and *The Irish Theological Quarterly*.

St Muredach's Cathedral, Ballina

In the lead-up to Catholic Emancipation and the erasing of restrictive laws on the building of Catholic places of worship, Killala diocese, one of the poorest in terms of resources and population, embarked on the massive project of building a new cathedral to replace the stone and thatch structure in Chapel Lane, which had served since 1740.

The project was first envisaged by the elderly Bishop Peter Waldron (1814-35), but taken vigorously in hand by his coadjutor, Bishop John MacHale, who succeeded him for a short time before becoming Archbishop of Tuam.

In 1831 the first Mass was celebrated within the rough-hewn shell of the new cathedral. The architect was Dominick Madden, who designed Tuam cathedral. Because of financial restraints and the disruption caused by the Famine, several modifications of the design had to be made. It was not until 1853, some twenty-three years after the roofing of the main building, that work on the spire resumed. The entire work on the cathedral was completed in 1892.

The glory of the edifice is in the interior ceiling and overall design, modelled on the vaulting and ribbing of the Church of Santa Maria Sopra Minerva in Rome. The contract for the groining, plastering and stucco work was awarded to Arthur Canning, who undertook to have the bosses at the intersection of the rib mouldings, the centre over the intersections of the nave and transepts, the busts at the intersections of the groins of the naves and side isles, and the crochets over the eastern windows 'executed by the first artists in the Kingdom'. How well he succeeded can be seen in the much-admired plasterwork of the cathedral ceiling, enhanced by the colour schemes and mosaics. The windows in the cathedral are the artistic treasuries of the building, all being the work of the Meyer studios of Munich, whose premises were destroyed by the Allied bombings in World War II.

One of the Millennium projects of the diocese, now in progress, is a complete renovation and refurbishment of the cathedral, which is scheduled for completion before Easter 2000.

Includes portions of Counties Mayo and Sligo

Killala

...indow in gable of Tirrane Church,
...rish of Kilmore Erris

...e window was executed by Christopher
...mbell of Dublin in 1962.

...nels: (Left to right) Naomh Íde ag
...gasc Bréanainn (St Ita instructing
...endan); Bréanainn agus an Míol Mór
...rendan and the Sea Beast); Bréanainn
...mramhach (Brendan the Voyager);
...lte Inis Ghlóire roimh Bhréanainn
...is Glóire welcomes Brendan);
...isreachadh Naomh Bréanainn (The
...nsecration of Brendan).

Diocese of
Killala

HISTORY OF THE DIOCESE

IN THE YEAR 1111 the Diocese of Killala was created and its boundaries delineated by the Synod of Rathbreasail. At the Synod of Kells in 1152 the boundaries were revised and confirmed.

The first Bishop of Killala mentioned in Roman records was Donatus O'Bechdha: his possession of the diocese was confirmed by Pope Innocent III in a rescript dated 30 March 1198. This records the transfer of ancient churches, monasteries and church properties to the jurisdiction of the diocesan bishop. In the process it provides a record of placenames in the diocese. *Insula Gedig*, for example, is Iniskea, an island in Blacksod Bay. *Inisgluairibrandani* is Inisglora of Brendan. The original monastery on this island was said to be founded by St Brendan.

In the twelfth century, three of the oldest native Irish monasteries were ordered to adopt the Rule of the Canons of St Augustine: Cross Abbey (which had been transferred from Inisglora to Kilmore Erris); Errew in Lough Conn and Aughris in Tireragh (said to have been founded from Inismurray by St Molaise in 571).

In the Middle Ages monasteries in the diocese included the three just mentioned, together with Rathfran, Ardnaree, Rosserk, Moyne and Bofeenaun. In the fifteenth century, Bishop Bernard O'Conaill (1432-61) involved himself in the Franciscan reform of the monasteries. Rosserk refused to reform and he supported the building of Moyne. This period was one of internecine conflict, with churches despoiled and ravaged. In fact O'Conaill himself was killed by the brother of a disaffected priest.

In the Reformation period, great efforts were made to establish English rule along the western seaboard and conflict with the religious authorities was part and parcel of that reality. On a trumped-up charge, Bishop Redmund O'Gallagher, a thorn in the side of the authorities, was imprisoned and banished from the diocese.

In 1566 he presided over a synod held to promulgate the decrees of the Council of Trent.

A biography of Bishop Francis Kirwan, who was appointed in 1645, gives a good insight into the diocese in the middle of the seventeenth century. He was one of the four bishops representing the Irish bishops at the Confederation of Kilkenny. He introduced a small catechism and had plans to set up a craft school. But then Cromwell came and the bishop lost his residence in Killala and went into hiding in a mice-invested room, where he said Mass on a chest. Later he returned in disguise to his native Galway. In June 1654 he was taken into custody with thirty priests, and after fourteen months he was deported to Nantes in France.

Tadhg O'Rourke, a Franciscan friar, was bishop from 1707 to 1739. In a letter to Rome he reported that the diocese had twenty-two parishes but only sixteen parish priests. The Catholic flock was numerous but they lived in direst poverty because the fertile lands had been confiscated and Catholics were forced to live in mountains and bogs.

In the time of Bishop Dominic Bellew (1779-1812) Ballina became the ecclesiastical centre of the diocese. When the French landed at Killala he kept a low profile, even though his brother joined the French forces and was killed. Bellew was involved in the two great issues of this time, the founding of Maynooth College and the struggle for Catholic Emancipation. In 1825 John MacHale, later Archbishop of Tuam, became coadjutor to Bishop Thomas Waldron, who assigned to him a project first proposed in 1820: building a new cathedral to replace the old thatched church built about 1740. The first Mass was said in the new building in autumn 1831. The interior was left unfinished because of lack of funds. No work was done again until the 1840s. In 1846 the onset of the Great Famine put a halt to further work; all church resources had to be devoted to the alleviation of hunger. The cathedral was not completed until 1892.

Killala diocese, which spans north Mayo and west Sligo, suffered terribly in the Great Famine. In 1847 a Mayo road inspector reported that he had secured the burial of 140 bodies which he found lying by the wayside, while in the same year fourteen schooners left Westport laden with wheat and oats. The *Sligo Champion* of 26 February 1847 reported 'Every hour the calamity is increasing.. hundreds of unfortunate creatures have within the last week, died of starvation. They were hurried to the grave coffinless and shroudless, so great is the mortality that the ancient customs are forgotten'. By 1851 a million had perished in Ireland and another million had emigrated.

After a short period of growth in the 1970s, when 20,000 emigrants returned to Connacht, rural communities in the west continued to decline. In the sixty-five years up to 1991, Connacht and Donegal lost one fifth of its population. In the Diocese of Killala there were villages and townlands where the total population between the ages of twenty and thirty-five could be counted on the fingers of one hand. Between 1986 and 1991 the rate of net emigration from the west more than doubled, while births more than halved.

In 1991 the western bishops launched an initiative called 'Developing the West Together'. This led to mass meetings in the western dioceses. In Killala over 500 attended a conference in Ballina and over 200 in Belmullet. Out of these meetings grew 'core groups', which had an important input into an EU-funded study of the west of Ireland called for by the bishops. This study resulted in the publication of the report *Crusade for Survival*.

The process generated by the bishops' initiative resulted in a number of important developments, among them the establishment by the bishops of the Council for the West, a Government task force that published 'Report on *Crusade for Survival*', and the establishment by the Government on 1 February 1999 of the statutory body called The Western Development Commission.

LACE OF PILGRIMAGE

Moyne Abbey

Once the primal abbey of the Franciscans of the reformed observance, the beautifully sited Moyne Abbey on the banks of the Moy has been chosen as the place of the Millennium Pilgrimage for the Diocese of Killala.

Following a series of local devotions at traditional shrines and holy places, pilgrims from all the parishes will converge on Moyne to mark the Jubilee and a monastic connection that goes back over five hundred years.

Moyne was dedicated in 1462 by Donagh O'Conor, Bishop of Killala, and at the height of its influence was a religious centre for aspiring monks. It housed fifty friars, including priests, professors, students and lay brothers and had a famous library. In its crypts were buried many of the great families of Tirawley and Tireragh – the O'Dowds, the Burkes, the Barretts and the Lynotts.

Its roofless walls also contained some of the most violent crimes of the Elizabethan campaign of suppression. In 1578 a detachment of soldiers from Sir Edward Fitton, the Governor of Connaught, invaded the monastery and the monks fled out to sea. They left behind an elderly lay brother who had volunteered to keep an eye on the soldiers, and who felt because of his venerable age that he would be safe, as he posed no threat to the invaders. The soldiers plundered all before them and, then pillaging the church, simply cut down the old man as he tried to protect the altar. The monks on their return found the body sprawled across the sanctuary steps.

The following year the monastery was again pillaged on the pretext of a plot being hatched there against the Queen. The soldiers captured a layman, Felim O'Hara, and threatened to kill him if he did not confess to the 'treason'. He asked to be allowed to confess to the prior and, when he had done so, the soldiers hanged him. Then they tortured the friar to get him to reveal the contents of the confession. They burst his skull under the pressure of a rope and stick, exposing his brain. The martyred monk was John O'Dowd, and his death on 9 June 1579 is remembered locally, as well as that of the layman Felim O'Hara.

Moyne, on its official dissolution, was given under Cromwell to Sir Arthur Gore. The Lindsay family came into possession of it and, with the demolition of the roof, are reported to have sold the huge abbey bell, a gift of the Queen of Spain, for the reputed sum of £700. Moyne was later owned by Kirkwood of Bartra Island, and in 1975 came into the possession of the Board of Works as a National Monument – as did its sister abbey of Rosserk.

The gift of the bell from Spain was one indication of the active trade carried on between the locality and the Continent. The Moy pooled outside the windows of the abbey and ships anchored there to reprovision.

In 1617, after its suppression, Father Donatus Mooney visited the site and left this written record: 'The situation is most pleasant, the building commodious, and constructed almost entirely of polished oolite stone. The gardens and the small grazing grounds are fenced with a strong stone wall. Inside the cloister itself, a stone spout draws water from the ground, which passes through the rooms and provides water for the use of the friars at six or seven points; then it passes to the sea, turning two grinding mills on the way'.

He goes on to describe the method of construction, in which the cement is made from seashells. The massive square tower of this finely preserved monastery is 90 feet high and commands a magnificent view of the Atlantic and the mountains of Donegal, Tireragh and Tirawley. The rich display of ornamentation in the tracery of the windows and on the pillars of the cloister speak of the fine crafts of the builders and make Moyne the gem of monastic preservations now in the care of the Board of Works.

The diocesan Jubilee Committee, neighbouring parishes, local landowners, the Board of Works, Killala diocesan clergy and religious, and local authorities are co-operating in preparing the monastery for the Jubilee Pilgrimage, which will feature the return of the Franciscans to their former abbey on that day.

The site has a particular link with St Muredach's Cathedral, now being renovated for the Jubilee, in that the stone used in the building of the cathedral (1829) was cut from the Moyne quarry adjoining the abbey, and ferried upstream to provide the first Catholic cathedral in the diocese after three hundred years of suppression.

Diocese of
Killaloe

Most Rev William Walsh DD

Willie Walsh is a native of Roscrea, Co Tipperary. He was educated at Corville National School, Roscrea and St Flannan's College, Ennis. He studied for the priesthood at St Patrick's College, Maynooth and the Irish College, Rome, and was ordained in Rome in 1959. After ordination, he completed his studies in Canon Law at the Lateran University in Rome. On his return to Ireland he taught for a year at Coláiste Einde, Galway, and he joined the staff of St Flannan's College, Ennis in 1963. In 1988 he was appointed curate at Ennis cathedral and became administrator there in 1990. He has been pastorally involved with ACCORD (formerly the Catholic Marriage Advisory Council) since its foundation in the Killaloe diocese and has worked with marriage tribunals at diocesan, regional and national levels. He has pursued a life-long interest in sport and has been involved in coaching hurling teams at college, club and county grades. He was ordained Bishop of Killaloe on 2 October 1994.

Cathedral of Sts Peter and Paul, Ennis

The church that now serves as the cathedral of the Diocese of Killaloe was originally built to serve as the parish church of Ennis. The diocese had not had a permanent cathedral since the Reformation. In 1828, Francis Gore, a Protestant landowner, donated the site for the new Catholic church. Dominick Madden, who also designed the cathedrals in Ballina and Tuam, was chosen as the architect.

The construction of the new church was a protracted affair. Shortly after the work began, the project ran into financial difficulties and was suspended for three years. Aided by generous donations from local Protestants, including Sir Edward O'Brien of Dromoland and Vesey Fitzgerald, the work began again in 1831. Progress was slow throughout the 1830s and there were many problems. In September 1837 there was a serious accident on the site when the scaffolding collapsed, killing two and seriously

injuring two more. Finally, in 1842, the roof was on and the parish priest, Dean O'Shaughnessy, was able to say the first Mass inside the still-unfinished building.

On 26 February 1843, the new church was blessed and placed under the patronage of Saints Peter and Paul, by Bishop Patrick Kennedy. Fr Matthew, 'The Apostle of Temperance', preached the sermon.

Much still remained to be done on the project, but the Great Famine brought the work to a halt. After the Famine, the work recommenced. J. J. McCarthy, one of the leading church architects in nineteenth-century Ireland, was commissioned to oversee the interior decoration of the building. Much of this is still visible, including the internal pillars and arches and the organ gallery.

A local committee decided in 1871 to complete the tower and spire, but owing to financial difficulties, it was not until 23 October 1874 that the final stone was put in place.

In 1889 Dr Thomas McRedmond was appointed coadjutor bishop and he was consecrated in 1890. He had full charge

of the diocese, owing to the illness of Bishop Flannery. Though he was already Parish Priest of Killaloe, the new bishop chose to make Ennis his home, remaining there after he succeeded to the office of diocesan bishop, on the death of Dr Flannery. The Parish Church of Sts Peter and Paul was thus designated the pro-cathedral of the diocese.

Major renovations were carried out in 1894. The present main entrance under the tower was constructed, a task that necessitated breaking through a six-foot thick wall. The building was also redecorated. The improvements were under the direction of Joshua Clarke, father of the stained-glass artist Harry Clarke. The large painting of the Ascension, which dominates the sanctuary, the work of the firm Nagle and Potts, was also installed at this time. The building remained largely unchanged for the next eighty years. A new sacristy and chapter room were added in the 1930s, as were the pipe organ and chapter stalls for the canons.

Another major renovation was carried out in 1973 to bring the building into line with the requirements of the Second Vatican Council. The architect for the work was Andrew Devane and the main contractors were Ryan Brothers, Ennis. The artistic adviser was Enda King. The building was reopened after six months in December 1973. *The Clare Champion* reported: 'The main features of the renovation included new altar, ambo, new tabernacle on granite pillar, baptismal font located near sanctuary, new flooring. New heating system, new amplification system and complete reconstruction of the sanctuary'.

In 1990, 163 years after work on the building began, Bishop Harty named it his cathedral. The solemn dedication of the cathedral and the altar took place on 18 November 1990. A fire at a shrine in the cathedral in October 1995 caused serious internal damage. The sanctuary had to be rebuilt and the building redecorated. The restoration was celebrated with Solemn Evening Prayer in November 1996.

and the doors were locked against him. For a while after the eviction, Fr Meehan said Mass in the open air, beneath the tilted shafts of two farmers' carts, over which large sheets were thrown to protect the altar. Then one day when he was in Kilkee, he got an idea, which resulted in the building of the 'Ark' by Owen Collins of Carrigaholt. After that, each Sunday, what was undoubtedly the smallest chapel in the world was placed on the green patch at the crossroads leading to the quay at Kilbaha and the people gathered round in the open air for Mass in good weather or bad.

Within a few years the 'Ark' received a lot of publicity, and this was of considerable help in ensuring that a site was eventually granted at Moneen in 1857. Soon afterwards, on 12 July of that year, the foundation stone of the 'Star of the Sea' Church was blessed by Bishop Daniel Vaughan, assisted by Bishop Whelan of Bombay. As the work on the building went ahead, Fr Meehan went to London collecting funds. A year later the new church was ready and the dedication took place on 10 October 1858. On the day of celebration, the presence of the 'Ark' near the door of the new church was a concrete reminder of the difficult struggle Fr Meehan had to wage to provide a church for the people of Kilbaha. The 'Ark' stands there to this day.

The Little Ark of Kilbaha

In the early 1850s a determined effort was made by the local land agent to get the people of the parishes of Moyarta and Kilballyowen to turn their backs on the Catholic faith. He concentrated his efforts on the Kilbaha area, as there was no church west of Cross. Fr Michael Meehan, who was refused a building site, celebrated Mass in a small farmhouse. When two adjoining houses became vacant because of emigration, he purchased them and, having knocked the wall between them, he had a rough-and-ready chapel for his congregation of 300. Within a month he got notice to quit

Diocese of
Killaloe

HISTORY OF THE DIOCESE

THE DIOCESE of Killaloe was established by the Synod of Rathbreasail in 1111. It is not clear what boundaries the diocese had at that time. However, when the Synod of Kells took place in 1152, the territory that currently forms the Diocese of Killaloe made up three separate dioceses, Killaloe (Cill Dá Lua), Roscrea (Ros Cré) and Scattery (Inis Cathaigh). Within a hundred years, the three were one and the Diocese of Killaloe adopted more or less the same boundaries that it has today.

Before the establishment of formal territorial dioceses at the Synod of Rathbreasail, the Church in Ireland was based largely around the monasteries, and many abbots were also bishops. The Diocese of Killaloe takes its name from a church erected in honour of Saint Molua at Killaloe. Molua died in the early seventh century. Some years later, St Flannan, acknowledged to be the first Bishop of Killaloe, lived there. St Senan was first Bishop and Abbot of Inis Cathaigh, off the west coast of Clare, near Kilrush. St Cronan, who died around 665, founded the monastery of Roscrea. Many other monks of this period are also venerated locally as saints, including Brendan of Birr, Caimin of Iniscealtra and Ruadhán of Lorrha.

Of the early Bishops of Killaloe after Rathbreasail, Constantine O'Brien (a direct descendant of Brian Boru) is the most noteworthy. He attended both the Third Lateran Council in 1179 and the Fourth Lateran Council in 1215. Cornelius Ryan OFM, who was bishop from 1576 to 1617, aided the Earl of Desmond's rebellion in 1579. He helped get support for the Catholic rebels from both Pope Gregory XIII and King Philip II of Spain. He died in exile in Lisbon, Portugal. John O'Molony was made bishop in 1671 and was instrumental in the foundation of the Irish College in Paris, where many Irish priests were educated during penal times. He was made Bishop of Limerick in 1689 and for

a while he presided over the two dioceses. He too was forced to flee from persecution and he died in France in 1702.

The great bishop of the eighteenth century was Michael Peter McMahon OP. He was bishop from 1765 until his death in 1807 at the age of ninety-seven. During his episcopate, many of the Penal Laws, which discriminated against Catholics, were relaxed and Catholics became more widely accepted in public life. Bishop Michael Flannery served from 1859 to 1891. However, owing to bad health he lived in Paris for most of that period. During this time Killaloe had three coadjutor bishops – Nicholas Power, James Ryan and Thomas McRedmond. Bishop Ryan moved the episcopal seat to Ennis and the new parish church became the pro-cathedral of the diocese. McRedmond eventually succeeded as bishop in his own right.

There have been four Bishops of Killaloe during this century. Michael Fogarty served for fifty-one years between 1904 and 1955. When he celebrated the Golden Jubilee of his episcopate in 1955 he was honoured by Pope Pius XII with the personal title of Archbishop. He was succeeded by Joseph Rodgers, who in turn was succeeded by Michael Harty in 1967. Bishop Harty presided over the considerable work of adapting the church in Killaloe in accordance with the decrees of the Second Vatican Ecumenical Council. Bishop Harty died in 1994 and was succeeded by Willie Walsh.

PLACE OF PILGRIMAGE

Monaincha – Móin na hInse
The Holy Island of Loch Cré

This little, now dry bog island, five mile east of Roscrea town, was once the thirty-first Wonder of the World and Munster's most famous place of pilgrimage in the Middle Ages. Holy Island – as it is still called, although it has been drained for over two hundred years – was once the hermitage site of local saints, Molua of Kyle, Cronan of Ros Cré and Canice from Aghaboe in nearby Laois. Here, according to the Annals, Maelpatraic Ua Drugáin, 'paragon of the wisdom of the Irish, chief lector of Ard Mhaca', head o the council of the west of Europe in piety and devotion, died on his pilgrimage at the island of Loch Cré on 2 January 1138'.

On a Sunday in June in the early seventeenth century the lord deputy complained that over 15,000 people – 'and some say many more' – had gathered there as pilgrims, led by the martyred Blessed Conor Devany.

The twelfth-century Irish Roman-esque church, the tranquillity of the place and the atmosphere of spirituality that still permeates this venerable and ancient location make any visit to Monaincha memorable.

In 1607 Pope Paul V granted an indulgence to those visiting, asking them to pray for peace among princes. Say a prayer there sometime for peace in our own land. Just as at Clonmacnois, 'here the very stones speak'.

Thou sacred and so holy
Honoured isle,
Had wet, now arid feet
In thousand pilgrim tears.

Diocese of Kilmore

Most Rev Leo O'Reilly DD

Leo O'Reilly was born in the parish of Kill, Co Cavan, on 10 April 1944. In 1962 he entered Maynooth College to study for the priesthood. He graduated with a BSc in 1965 and with a BD in 1968. After ordination in 1969 he did the Higher Diploma in Education and was appointed as a teacher to St Patrick's College, Cavan. In 1976 he went to Rome for further studies in the Gregorian University. He was Director of Studies in the Irish College from 1978 to 1980. In 1981 he received a Doctorate in Theology from the Gregorian University for his thesis 'Word and Sign in the Acts of the Apostles: A Study in Lucan Theology'. The thesis was later published in the series *Analecta Gregoriana* of the Gregorian University Press. Upon his return to Ireland in 1981 he was appointed chaplain to the Community School, Bailieborough, Co Cavan. In 1988 he volunteered to go to Nigeria as a member of the Kilmore mission team, working with the Kiltegan Fathers in the Diocese of Minna. After some years in parish ministry he was appointed to the staff of St Paul's Missionary Seminary, Abuja, to teach Scripture and to engage in the formation of Nigerian students for the missionary priesthood. When he returned to his diocese in 1995 he was appointed Parish Priest of Castletara. He was ordained Coadjutor Bishop of Kilmore on 2 February 1997. Upon the retirement of Bishop Francis MacKiernan, Bishop O'Reilly was installed as Bishop of Kilmore on 15 November 1998. Bishop O'Reilly is currently a member of the Episcopal Commissions on Education, Liturgy, and Research and Development, and a member of the Department of Theological Questions of the Irish Inter-Church Committee.

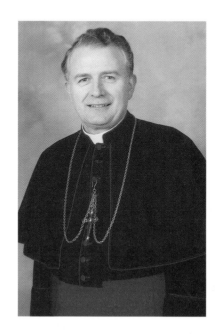

Cathedral of St Patrick and St Felim, Cavan

The original cathedral of the diocese was situated about four miles south of Cavan in the present parish of Kilmore. Some time in the sixth century, St Felim had established a church there. Bishop Andrew MacBrady (1445-55) rebuilt the ancient church of St Felim and received permission from Pope Nicholas V to raise it to the status of a cathedral. After the confiscation of the Cathedral of St Felim at Kilmore, the diocese had no cathedral for three hundred years. Bishop James Browne extended Cavan parish church and erected it into a cathedral in 1862. It was replaced by the new Cathedral of St Patrick and St Felim, built by Bishop Patrick Lyons in the years 1938-42. The architects were W. H. Byrne & Son and the contractors John Sisk & Son. The cathedral cost £209,000 and was opened and dedicated in 1942. It was consecrated in 1947.

The cathedral is neo-classical in style with a single spire rising to 230 feet. The portico consists of a tympanum supported by four massive columns of Portland stone with Corinthian caps. The tympanum figures of Christ, St Patrick and St Felim were executed by a Dublin sculptor, George Smith. The twenty-eight columns in the cathedral, the pulpit on the south side and all the statues are of Pavinazetto marble and came from the firm of Dinelli Figli of Pietrasanta in Italy.

The fine work of George Collie can be seen in the Stations of the Cross and in the mural of the Risen Christ on the wall of the apse. Directly above the mural are twelve small windows, showing the heads of the twelve apostles. The High Altar is of green Connemara marble and pink Middleton marble, while the altar rails are of white Carrara marble. The apse has two side-chapels on the north and two on the south. The Blessed Sacrament is now reserved in the south chapel closest to the altar. The six splendid stained-glass windows in the nave and one in the south transept came from the studios of Harry Clarke.

Stained-glass window, Cathedral of St Patrick and St Felim

This stained-glass window was executed by Harry Clarke. It depicts St Patrick and two princesses. It is one of a set of eight stained-glass windows that were installed in the cathedral in 1994 by the Abbey Stained-Glass Studios. They were originally commissioned for the Sacred Heart Convent, Leeson Street, Dublin, between 1919 and 1934. The other windows in the set depict the following:

- St Ann and the Holy Child Mary
- Blessed Sophie Barat
- St Francis Xavier with a group of Asian people
- St Charles Borromeo giving Holy Communion to the young Aloysius Gonzaga
- The Sacred Heart and St Margaret Mary Alacoque
- St Michael the Archangel
- Our Lady appearing to St Bernard.

Kilmore

Diocese of
Kilmore

HISTORY OF THE DIOCESE

THE DIOCESE of Kilmore has as its patron the sixth-century bishop, St Felim. Its boundaries, as established by the Synod of Kells, correspond with those of Breifne, the medieval kingdom of the O'Rourkes. In 1454 Bishop Andrew MacBrady petitioned Pope Nicholas V to raise the Church of St Feilimidh in the parish of Kilmore to the status of a cathedral and to erect a chapter of thirteen canons and two dignitaries. This cathedral, as well as the other churches in the diocese, passed into the hands of the Church of Ireland at the Reformation.

During the period of persecution, the Franciscan Bishop Richard Brady (1580-1607) was imprisoned three times and Blessed Conn O'Rourke, a native of Drumhaire, was martyred at Kilmallock in 1579, along with another son of Creevelea Abbey, the Franciscan Bishop of Mayo, Patrick O'Healey. Hugh O'Reilly became Bishop of Kilmore in 1626 but was transferred to Armagh in 1628. He worked hard for the success of the Confederation of Kilkenny. Eugene MacSweeney, a native of Donegal, succeeded Primate Hugh as Bishop of Kilmore and at one time was the only bishop in Ireland. He died in 1669 and the see was vacant for almost sixty years.

The years of the vacancy were particularly difficult. The diocese was ruled by vicars, who found it hard to maintain discipline. In 1715 the parish priests of the diocese asked Rome to appoint Michael Smith as bishop. 'The diocese', they wrote, 'was more than forty-six years without a bishop to confer Orders and Confirmation and to settle with his authority the frequent disputes that arise. The clergy are in the greatest need. All the dignitaries of the Cathedral Chapter are dead and we alone are left, decrepit old men, no longer able to work in the vineyard'.

Religious toleration improved in the eighteenth century and Rome began again to appoint bishops in Ireland. Michael MacDonagh, a Dominican, was appointed to Kilmore in 1728. He was succeeded by another Dominican, Laurence Richardson, in 1747, and Andrew Campbell, an Armagh priest, followed in 1753. All three were non-resident and visited the diocese for short periods only. The transfer of Denis Maguire, a Franciscan, from Dromore to Kilmore in 1770 gave a new stability. He began the process of rebuilding both discipline and churches.

James Browne, a priest of Ferns and Professor of Scripture in Maynooth, was appointed to Kilmore in 1827 to meet the threat of the evangelicals. He lived until 1865 and was Kilmore's most outstanding bishop. He reformed the diocese, continued the building of churches and schools, recruited more vocations to the priesthood, founded the first diocesan college in 1839, and at the time of his death the modern Diocese of Kilmore had taken shape. Nicholas Conaty, who succeeded Browne, continued the work of church building. Some of the finest churches in the diocese date from that period and are the work of the talented Cavan architect, William Hague Jr. He was also the architect of St Patrick's College, Cavan. Bishop Patrick Lyons (1937-49) built the Cathedral of St Patrick and St Felim. Bishop Austin Quinn (1950-72) established secondary schools in Bailieboro, Ballinamore, Ballyjamesduff, Cootehill and Manorhamilton. Bailieborough later became a community school and Cootehill and Manorhamilton comprehensive schools.

PLACE OF PILGRIMAGE

St Kilian's Shrine at Mullagh

St Kilian was born about AD 640 in the townland of Cloughballybeg in the parish of Mullagh in Co Cavan, near the site of the holy well that bears his name. He was educated at one of the great monastic schools of the time, Fore or Clonmacnois, and he later made his way to Roscarbery. He founded the monastery of Kilmackillogue in the parish of Tuosist near Kenmare and from there in 686 sailed with eleven companions by way of the Rhine and Maine to Franconia in Germany.

According to tradition these Irish monks planted the cross on a hill called the Kreuzberg overlooking Wurzburg. Kilian converted Duke Gosbert and thousands of Franconians, so that he became known as the Apostle of Franconia. However, Gosbert's wife became his sworn enemy and finally succeeded in having him murdered in 689 with his companions Totnan and Colonat. Their bodies were only discovered in 752, buried in a stable. The church to which their relics were transferred has been a place of pilgrimage ever since.

Kilian's birthplace and the holy well associated with it, Tubberkilahan, in the parish of Mullagh, have also been a place of pilgrimage for centuries. A well-attended 'pattern' with music and dancing was held there annually on 8 July down to the early nineteenth century. Because of drunkenness and fighting during the 'pattern', it was suppressed by Fr Felix McCabe, who was parish priest of Mullagh from 1794 to 1816, but the people who lived nearby continued to whitewash the stones and decorate them with flowers. In more recent times the custom of visiting the well on the eve of the feast of St Kilian has been revived.

In 1991 Bishop Paul Werner Scheele of Wurzburg brought back relics of St Kilian to Mullagh and St Kilian's shrine in Mullagh is a place of pilgrimage for, among others, people from Wurzburg, following in the footsteps of Father Maas, a Bavarian priest who first came as a pilgrim to St Kilian's birthplace in 1970.

Diocese of
Limerick

Most Rev Donal Murray DD

Bishop Murray was born in 1940. He attended Blackrock College, Dublin, obtained his BA and Masters in Philosophy at University College, Cork, his BDiv at Maynooth and his Licence and Doctorate in Theology at the University of St Thomas, Rome.

He was ordained a priest on 22 May 1966 and has lectured extensively in Theology and ethical issues. He lectured at Mater Dei Institute in 1969 and was Professor of Moral Theology at Clonliffe College in 1970. From 1973 to 1982 he lectured on Cathechetics in University College, Dublin, and from 1978 to 1982 he lectured on Medical Ethics in UCD.

Bishop Murray is a well-known and respected author in the areas of theology, ethics and social issues, having written three books and numerous articles, booklets and pamphlets.

In 1982, at the age of forty-one, he was appointed Auxiliary Bishop of Dublin. At that time he was the youngest member of the Irish hierarchy.

His advice and opinion is highly valued. He served as adviser to the Irish representatives at the World Synod of Bishops in 1977. He is a member of the Vatican's Council for Culture and of four Episcopal Commissions. He is the moving force in the Joint Commission for Bio-Ethical Issues for the Bishops' Conferences of Ireland, England, Wales and Scotland.

On 24 March 1996 he was installed as Bishop of Limerick.

St John's Cathedral, Limerick

Since the twelfth century, a church dedicated to St John has stood in the area of Limerick city known as Garryowen. The earliest reference to the first church comes from the year 1205 when the Cathedral Chapter of the Diocese of Limerick was founded by Bishop Donatus O'Brien, Bishop of Limerick from 1195 to 1207. In the document of foundation, the revenues from the Church of St John were given to the Archdeacon of Limerick.

This medieval church was replaced by a penal church, which in turn was supplanted by the parish church of St John in the middle of the eighteenth century. With an increase in population in the area around Garryowen, it was decided to build a new church to accommodate the estimated 15,000 parishioners of St John's. An appeal for funds was so well received that the decision was made to abandon the plans for a parish church and build a cathedral for the diocese instead.

Designed by Philip Charles Hardwick, a contemporary and associate of Pugin, St John's Cathedral is revival Gothic in the early English style. It was opened for worship in 1861 and consecrated in 1894 by Cardinal Logue. The spire, standing at 308 feet, 3 inches, is the tallest in Ireland and was built between 1878 and 1883.

Includes the greater part of County Limerick, part of County Clare and one townland in County Kerry

Treasures of the Diocese of Limerick

Black Book of Limerick
This is a manuscript, the earliest part of which contains a compilation of documents once held in the archives of the bishops of Limerick and which dates from around 1362. Later additions date from the fifteenth and early nineteenth centuries.

White's Manuscript
This is a compilation of the Annals of Limerick (in manuscript) made by Father White (1715-68), Parish Priest of St Mary's Parish, Limerick city.

Statue of the Immaculate Mother (left)
This statue by the Italian sculptor Giovanni Benzoni was presented to the cathedral by William Maunsell, Lord Emly, in 1861.

O'Dea Mitre and Crozier
These items date from the early fifteenth century. The O'Dea Crozier is the earliest piece of medieval Irish art in Church possession and is currently on display in the Hunt Museum in Limerick.

Ardagh Chalice
This item was found in Co Limerick and is on display in the National Museum, Dublin.

Diocese of
Limerick

History of the Diocese

Though the shadowy figure of the seventh-century St Munchin is its patron, the Diocese of Limerick actually dates from the twelfth century, when its boundaries were laid down at the Synod of Rathbreasail. It is unlikely that any diocesan structure had existed prior to that time and the local bishops would simply have been members of the monastic communities in the area. While they would have had some prestige, it was the abbots who held power and were the administrators of the Church system. The Vikings were primarily responsible for the establishment of a diocesan system in Ireland and the city of Limerick played a leading role in that development through the work of its first bishop, Gilbert. He was initially consecrated as a bishop for the city and subsequently took charge of the diocese when it was formed in the year 1111. One of the most remarkable features of the diocese is that its boundaries have not changed significantly since that time and were in turn based on an older territorial division, a Munster sub-kingdom ruled by the Uí Fidgente kings.

On his death in 1145 Gilbert was succeeded by Bishop Patrick, who probably took his name at his consecration and may have been of Viking ancestry, as indeed Gilbert probably was. The next bishop, of whom we have record, is Brictius. He took part in the Synod of Cashel in 1172 and also represented Limerick at the Third Lateran Council in 1179. It is of interest that he travelled to Rome with St Laurence O'Toole, the first canonised Irish saint.

The Black Book of Limerick, a manuscript transcription of various medieval documents relating to the diocese, provides valuable information for that period. In 1201 an enquiry was held into the ecclesiastical property of the diocese, conducted by a jury made up equally of Irish, Norman and Viking members, indicating the cosmopolitan nature of the diocese at that time. This invaluable list of early thirteenth-century churches is printed and discussed in

Begley's history of the diocese. In a taxation return for 1302 we learn that the diocese had been divided into deaneries, and a proxy tax of 1418 gives another list of churches, which affords a valuable comparison with the situation in 1201. It is to Cornelius O'Dea, bishop from 1400 to 1426, that we are indebted for the two great treasures of the diocese, the O'Dea Mitre and Crozier. He was also responsible for the compilation of the Black Book, which was returned to its rightful home in the diocese during the recent episcopate of the late Bishop Newman.

At the Reformation, Bishop John Quin, a Dominican priest from Kilmallock friary, accepted the limited changes of King Henry VIII, as his successor Bishop William Casey did the Lutheran system of Edward VI. Following the restoration of papal links under Queen Mary, Casey was dismissed, and Hugh Lacy, a member of the prominent Co Limerick Anglo-Norman family, was appointed. He remained in office until 1571, when he was removed by Queen Elizabeth and William Casey was restored as the new Anglican bishop. It is from this date that the final cleavage occurred and henceforth there were to be separate bishops for the Catholic and Anglican dioceses. Bishop Lacy died in 1580 and two years later the Holy See appointed Cornelius O'Boyle as bishop. He was then in Spain, where he appears to have remained until his death in 1597.

Limerick was without a bishop for a further twenty years until Richard Arthur, who had been vicar general, was appointed. On his death in 1646 he was buried in St Mary's Cathedral, which had come into Catholic hands during the Confederate wars of the 1640s. His successor, Dr Edmund O'Dwyer, undertook a reorganisation of the diocese and his report to Rome in 1649 gives a valuable insight into the situation at that time. He survived the siege of the city by Ireton in 1650 and after the surrender escaped to Brussels, where he died in 1654. The difficult period of the Cromwellian regime was succeeded by a more tolerant approach after the restoration of Charles II. In 1677 a new

bishop, Dr James Dowley, was appointed. Two years later he sent an optimistic report to Rome on the state of the diocese. Education was flourishing, with schools in every parish and a weekly sermon on Sundays. He established two confraternities in the city, visited each parish in the diocese and ordained priests regularly. Even during the brief persecution occasioned by the Popish plot scare, he was not hindered in his episcopate. He lived until 1685, which saw the Catholic monarch James II ascend the throne. Dr John O'Moloney was transferred from the See of Killaloe to Limerick in 1689, but he left for the Continent before the 1690 siege and the administration of the diocese was in the hands of his cousin, Dr Matthew Moloney, and Dr James Stritch, vicars general, during the tumultuous period of the sieges and the treaty of 1691.

The diocese was again without a bishop during the early years of the eighteenth century, when much anti-Catholic legislation was passed by the Irish parliament. A new bishop, Dr Cornelius O'Keeffe, was eventually appointed in 1720 and he managed to administer the diocese successfully despite the legal restrictions. In the 1780s, during the episcopate of Dr Conway, a report to Rome on the state of the diocese shows that the Church did not suffer as severely under the penal legislation as is often supposed. The diocese was divided into four decanates, each presided over by a vicar forane, who held a conference of its priests once a month. The forty parishes of the diocese each had a chapel with at least basic facilities and there was no shortage of priests. The Mass Rocks of popular folklore were clearly not the normal location for the Mass. The chapels in the five city parishes were larger and more ornate. There were no convents of nuns and the report notes with concern the refusal of some clerical students to return to the diocese after their ordination at continental colleges. In 1825 Dr John Ryan from Tipperary was appointed coadjutor bishop, with the right of succession to the elderly and infirm Bishop Charles Tuohy. The grant of

Catholic Emancipation in 1829 revitalised the Church in the diocese and during the long episcopate of Bishop Ryan and those of his successors, Bishops Butler and O'Dwyer, there were major programmes of church building, parish reorganisation, liturgical innovation and spiritual renewal. Their record of achievement and commitment to the diocese has been continued and expanded by their twentieth-century successors – in our own time, by Bishops Murphy, Newman and Murray – in the see established by Gilbert more than eight centuries ago.

PLACE OF PILGRIMAGE

Killeedy and St Ita

The ruins of Killeedy Church and the site of the ancient monastery of St Ita continue to this day to be a place of particular devotion and pilgrimage for the people in the surrounding country-side and beyond. On 15 January each year large crowds attend Mass in the two churches of the parish and do their 'Rounds' as they celebrate the feastday of their local saint and patroness of the Diocese of Limerick.

Ita was born in the Déise country (the present Co Waterford) in the sixth century. It was written of her that 'from the font of baptism she was filled with the Holy Spirit'. At first she was called Deirdre. Because of her great thirst for God and the things of God, her name was changed to Ita.

Ita's father had very definite plans for her long-term security and welfare, but Ita herself wanted to put God first in her life and she placed her confidence in prayer and fasting. Soon her father relented and consented to her serving God wherever she wished. We are told that Ita left her home with great feelings of joy and gratitude to God. She travelled west to the present Co Limerick and at a place called Cluain Credail at the foot of Sliabh Luchra she decided to settle and found her Christian Community.

There she devoted her life to prayer and the care of all who came to her. Her most popular title was 'the foster mother of the saints'. Her best-known fosterling was St Brendan of Kerry and Clonfert.

One day at prayer, as she thanked God for all his kindness to her, she experienced a great desire for the privilege of nursing the child Jesus. Her wish was granted. This wondrous experience is recorded in the poem 'Íosagán':

Íosagán
An leanbh oilim im dhíseartán
Do chléireach cad ab fhiú líon séad?
Is bréag gach ní ach Íosagán.

An leanbh althramaim im thig
Ní leanbh duine dhothíosaigh –
Íosa mar aon le fearaibh Neimhe
Lem chroí-se' bhíonn gach aon oíche.

Clann mac prionsa, clann mac rí,
Im thír má thagann chugham gach lá
Ní huathu shílim sochar:
Is dealraithí liom Íosagán.

* * *

Little Jesus
is nursed by me in my little hermitage.
Though a cleric should have great wealth,
all is deceit but little Jesus.

The nursing (fostering) done by me in my house
is not the nursing of one of low degree.
Jesus with the people of heaven
is by my heart every night….

The sons of nobles, the sons of kings,
although they come into my country,
not from them do I expect profit,
dearer to me is little Jesus….

In this poem Ita uses the word 'díseartán', the diminutive of the term 'dísert' to describe where she lived. The word díseart, anglicised Dysert, meant a solitary place, *locus desertus*. It was the term used for a retreat or hermitage where a holy person lived the Gospel in the early days of Christianity in Ireland.

The tenderness of St Luke's Gospel is again evoked in a story of her familiarity with the Trinity. One day when she was asleep, Ita saw an angel of the Lord approach her and give her three precious stones. On awakening she recalled the dream but did not know its significance. Then an angel appeared to her and said, 'why are you wondering about the dream? These three precious stones signify the coming of the Blessed Trinity to you, Father, Son and Holy Spirit. So always in your sleep and vigils the angels of God and holy visions will come to you, for you are a temple of God in body and soul'.

Ita would retire frequently to give herself entirely to prayer and contemplation and particularly to meditation on the mysteries of the most Holy Trinity.

Saints who were held in great affection by the people sometimes had the word 'mo' or 'my' prefixed to their name. In this way Íde became MoÍde, contracted in the spoken language to Míde. So as well as the parish called Killeedy (Cill Íde), the Church of Ita, there is a neighbouring parish called Kilmeedy (Cill Míde), the Church of My Ita. There is a holy well in the West Limerick parish of Knockaderry known as Tobar Míde.

The ancient parish of Killeedy was much more extensive than the present-day parish. So it is clear that the influence of Ita spread far and wide. With Mainchín (the little monk), in English St Munchin, she became the patron of the diocese.

The monastery of Killeedy was raided on several occasions and Viking attacks in the ninth century destroyed it. A Romanesque church was built on the site and this is now in ruins. A statue of St Ita holding the church in her left arm has been erected and flowers are regularly placed on the spot known as St Ita's grave.

St Ita and her community left a memory of great faith in and awareness of the Blessed Trinity, a tender love of the child Jesus and a practical love of children and young people as members of God's family. Killeedy continues to be a place of prayer and spiritual nourish-ment as Ita's memory renews the hearts of pilgrims thirsting for peace and the loving kindness of the heart of our God.

The Irish version of 'Íosagán' is taken from *Rí na nUile* (Sáirséal agus Dill, Baile Átha Cliath, 1964). The English version is from *Irish Catholic Spirituality* (The Columba Press, 1998).

Diocese of
Meath

Most Rev Michael Smith DCL, DD

Dr Smith, a native of Liss in Oldcastle parish, was born in June 1940. He was educated at the Gilson schools, St Finian's and the Irish College, Rome, where he was ordained in 1963. He studied philosophy and theology and received a Doctorate in Canon Law at the Lateran University in 1966. During his time in Rome he attended all sessions of the Second Vatican Council as part of a small group entrusted with the task of preparing the official record of the Council.

His first appointment was as assistant priest in Clonmellon parish in 1967. He served as chaplain of St Loman's from 1968 to 1974 and was diocesan secretary from 1968 to 1984, whilst also serving as chaplain to Sacred Heart Hospital in Mullingar from 1975 until 1984. In June 1970 he was appointed as the first executive secretary of the Irish Bishops' Conference, and on his appointment as bishop in 1984 he became episcopal secretary to the Conference, succeeding Dr McCormack. He was executive secretary of the Committee of Bishops and of the National Committee entrusted with the task of organising Pope John Paul II's visit to Ireland in 1979.

Following Dr McCormack's illness in Lourdes, Dr Smith was appointed Auxiliary Bishop of Meath and titular Bishop of Leges on 28 November 1983. His episcopal ordination took place in the Cathedral of Christ the King on 29 January 1984, by Cardinal Tomás Ó Fiaich, assisted by Dr Alibrandi, Papal Nuncio to Ireland and Bishop Cahal Daly, Bishop of Down and Connor.

On Thursday, 13 October 1988, Dr Smith was appointed Coadjutor Bishop of Meath, and in May 1990, on the resignation of Bishop McCormack, he was appointed Bishop of Meath.

Edward Smith Crucifix in St Mary's Church, Navan

In 1791, as the Penal Laws were beginning to come to an end, a new church was built in Navan, on the site of the present St Mary's. The merchants of Navan commissioned a crucifix from Edward Smith. Smith was a Meathman and may even have lived in Navan. He was the leading Irish sculptor of his day, and the crucifix was one of the finest pieces of religious art of the century. Before the crucifix was installed in Navan, it was exhibited in Dublin, where people had to pay sixpence to see it. A report in the *Dublin Evening Post* of 9 August 1792 reads as follows:

'An inimitably fine piece of sculpture is at present exhibited at the Dublin Museum, Mary Street. It is a crucifixion, large as life, from the chisel of Mr Smith – an Irish artist – who already stands eminently distinguished by the superior excellence of his productions in his professional line. To him, the city of Dublin owes the beautiful statue of Lucan at the Exchange, that of the Marquis of Buckingham, the emblematical figures of the new Custom House, the statues erected at the House of Lords etc.'

The carved wooden crucifix in St Mary's Church is one of the few ecclesiastical works done by Smith. Over the decades the work acquired some embellishments not least being painted. A moustache was added and the beard lengthened by using a white plaster. In 1973, Dr James White Director of the National Gallery, agreed to undertake a complete restoration of the work. The crucifix was then restored to St Mary's Church, where it hangs at the back of the High Altar. In recent times, a local artist, Patrick Reel, has painted a backdrop of Jerusalem, which enhances the visual impact of the crucifix.

Meath

athedral of Christ the King, Mullingar

the Penal Laws began to be relaxed, shop Patrick Plunkett was appointed shop of Meath in 1778. He was to end the next forty-nine years of his life storing and rebuilding the diocese. He d no cathedral, but providing one was t his immediate priority. Towards the d of his time as bishop, work began on e magnificent new Church of St Mary Navan. This was opened in 1830 and s considered the Cathedral Church of e Diocese. In 1870 Bishop Thomas lty decided to locate the bishop's idence in Mullingar, and the parish

church there was designated Cathedral Church of the Diocese. It had been built in 1828 but was quite small.

On his appointment as bishop in 1900, Matthew Gaffney called a public meeting to discuss the building of a cathedral for the Diocese of Meath. This meeting adopted the following resolution: 'The Diocese of Meath not having a cathedral nor the parish of Mullingar a suitable church, be it resolved that a church be built in Mullingar which will fulfil this double purpose'. A building fund was established, and £15,000 was subscribed at this first meeting – a very sizeable sum

at that time. It was not until the day of his consecration as bishop in 1929 that Thomas Melvyn was able to announce the decision to proceed with the project. Ralph A. Byrne, chief architect with William H. Byrne & Son, Dublin, prepared plans, which were accepted. Work began in 1932, and the Cathedral of Christ the King was opened for worship in September 1936. It was consecrated on 30 August 1939, the debt having been cleared. In recent years, a major renovation, including the replacement of the roof, has been completed.

Diocese of Meath

HISTORY OF THE DIOCESE

THE BOUNDARIES of the Diocese of Meath follow closely the boundaries of the territory of the High King of Ireland who resided at Tara and ruled over the Kingdom of Meath. They include Co Meath, most of Co Westmeath, a large part of Co Offaly, along with two parishes in Co Cavan and a small portion of Co Longford. The river Boyne is the dividing line, in the town of Drogheda, with the Archdiocese of Armagh.

The Diocese of Meath grew out of seven dioceses that were linked to major monastic sites. Surprisingly, Slane, where St Patrick began his mission in Ireland, was not one of these. Clonard was the first of the great teaching monasteries, and its founder, St Finian, became the patron of the diocese. At the Synod of Kells in 1152 the seven dioceses were reduced to three – Duleek, Clonard and Kells – on the understanding that over time these three would become one. This happened towards the end of the twelfth century, although documentary evidence for this decision, assumed to have been taken at Kells, is scant.

What is certain is that Bishop Simon Rochford (1192-1224) was the first bishop of the united diocese. He was buried in the abbey at Newtown, Trim. Ard-braccan, near Navan in Co Meath, and Killeen, also in Co Meath and residence of relatives of St Oliver Plunkett, were the places of residence of many of the bishops in pre-Reformation times. During penal times at least one bishop resided in Dublin, and when Bishop Patrick Plunkett began his long ministry of rebuilding the diocese in 1778 he decided to live in Navan. Bishop Cantwell, on his appointment as bishop in 1830, chose to live in Mullingar, but it was his successor, Bishop Thomas Nulty, who fixed the permanent residence of the bishop in Mullingar. He built Cathedral House in early 1870, and the then parish church of Mullingar was

given the status of cathedral. The decision to build a cathedral was taken by his successor, Bishop Matthew Gaffney, and the building fund for this project was started in 1900. Work began on the cathedal in 1932 and it was opened for worship in 1936.

When the Diocese of Clonmacnois was suppressed in 1729, its bishop, Stephen MacEgan, was transferred to Meath, and Clonmacnois joined to Meath. Some years later it was joined to the Diocese of Ardagh. Apart from this, the boundary of the diocese has not changed from the twelfth century to the present day.

Two people from the diocese who contributed greatly to the faith in Ireland, making the ultimate sacrifice of their lives, were St Oliver Plunkett from Loughcrew, Oldcastle, Co Meath and Blessed Margaret Ball (née Bermingham) from the Skryne area of Co Meath. Margaret Ball is to date the only Irish woman officially honoured by the Church since formal canonisation and beatification became part of the life of the Church towards the end of the first millennium.

PLACE OF PILGRIMAGE

The Hill of Slane

While there are many important sites in the diocese, such as Clonard, Kells and Durrow, all central to the development of the Church in Ireland, the one that attracts most interest is the Hill of Slane the site of St Patrick's first act when he came to Ireland as bishop.

Slane became a major monastic settlement, its founder being St Erc, who was also its first bishop. The monastery was plundered and destroyed on a number of occasions, especially during the twelfth century. In 1170 Diarmuid MacMurrough plundered and burned the monastery. It was replaced by a Franciscan friary, which lasted until it was destroyed by Cromwell. The ruins that can now be visited on the Hill date from 1512.

Each year a Mass is celebrated on the Hill, organised by the Capuchin Fathers the last inhabitants of the friary. The parish of Slane has for many years begun the Easter Vigil Ceremonies on the Hill with the lighting and blessing of the fire Major celebrations were held there in 1932 and again in 1961.

On Saturday, 24 June 2000, the Diocese of Meath will hold its principal Jubilee celebration on the Hill of Slane. Some participants in this celebration will be invited to walk from the mouth of the Boyne to Slane (following the journey St Patrick) or from Tara to Slane (following the journey of the people who went from the court of King Hugh to meet St Patrick at Slane).

Diocese of
Ossory

Most Rev Laurence Forristal DD

Laurence Forristal, son of William Forristal and Kathleen Phelan, was born in Jerpoint in the parish of Thomastown, Co Kilkenny, in 1931. He attended the national schools in Thomastown and later the Cistercian College in Roscrea, Co Tipperary.

As a seminarian in Clonliffe College, he studied philosophy at UCD. He completed his seminary formation at Propaganda Fide College, Rome, where he studied theology and was ordained priest for the Archdiocese of Dublin on 21 December 1955.

His first appointment in 1956 was as chaplain to the Dominican Convent, Sion Hill, Blackrock, Dublin, and priest-teacher in the Vocational School, Killester. After further studies in UCD and at the Gregorian University, Rome, he became assistant in the Chancellery, Archbishop's House, Dublin. At the same time he was chaplain, firstly to St Vincent's Orphanage, Glasnevin, and later to Highpark Convent, Drumcondra.

He was appointed curate in Raheny in 1967 and in 1974 he became administrator and later parish priest in Rivermount in the Finglas area. He was appointed Vicar General in the Archdiocese of Dublin in 1977.

On 20 January 1980 he was ordained Auxiliary Bishop of Dublin and Titular Bishop of Rotdon, and on 30 June 1981 he succeeded Bishop Peter Birch as Bishop of Ossory, his native diocese, having spent twenty-five years as a priest in the Archdiocese of Dublin.

St Mary's Cathedral, Kilkenny

It was only in the last decade of the twelfth century, during the episcopate of Felix O'Dulany, that Kilkenny became the seat of the Bishop of Ossory. The new cathedral, dedicated to St Canice, was begun early in the thirteenth century by Bishop Hugh de Rous and took over half a century to complete. During the period of the Confederation, it was David Rothe's cathedral church, and it was here that the aged bishop formally received the Papal Nuncio, Archbishop Rinuccini, in November 1645. With the coming of Cromwell, St Canice's reverted to Protestant hands and the Catholics had no cathedral. A small chapel in St Mary's parish – St James's Chapel, built in 1700 just outside St James's Gate – functioned as a cathedral and was in use up to 1857.

It was William Kinsella, appointed Bishop of Ossory in 1829, who initiated the building of St Mary's. William

Deane Butler, the architect for St Kieran's College and the parochial church of Ballyragget, was chosen to be the architect of St Mary's. His neo-Gothic style marked a new and ambitious phase in church architecture and reflected the newfound confidence of the Catholic community.

The site chosen was Burrell's Hall, which housed the first Catholic college founded in Ireland after the repeal of the law against Catholic schoolmasters in 1782. Subscribers from St Mary's parish pledged over £1,500, including £100 from Bishop Kinsella and £20 from Fr Theobald Matthew. Money was also raised from door and street collections, from the sale of site materials and from bank loans. Work was begun in April 1843. On 18 August the foundation stone was laid by Bishop Kinsella, assisted by the administrator, Fr Robert O'Shea, and others. When Bishop Kinsella died in December 1845, the walls were only seven feet high.

The new bishop, Edmond Walsh, aided by Robert O'Shea and a very active lay committee, continued the project. They kept it going right through the famine years, providing much-needed work locally. Collections were taken up in all the parishes of the diocese and bank loans were obtained on the securities of local merchants. The much-publicised sermon of Dr Patrick Murray of Maynooth also helped to raise funds. The cost of the original building is estimated at £25,000. The grand opening took place on 4 October 1857.

The cathedral was described as 'of pure Gothic design, built entirely of chiselled limestone and cruciform in shape'. The tower, originally designed for St Kieran's College, rises to a height of 186 feet. The high altar of Italian marble was purchased in Italy. The relics of Sts Cosmos and Damian and St Clement were brought from Rome. Those of St Victoria came later. A statue of Our Lady by Benzoni was commissioned by Bishop Walsh and stands in the remodelled sanctuary. The railings around the cathedral were added in 186

During Bishop Brownrigg's time, a new sacristy and chapter room were added and many other improvements were made. The centre porch and organ gallery were remodelled, heating was installed and new statues purchased. James Pearse, the father of Patrick and Willie, completed the marble altar rails and erected the altar to the Sacred Heart. About £8,000 was expended and the refurbished cathedral was reopened on 9 April 1899 in the presence of Cardinal Logue, Archbishop Walsh of Dublin and many other dignitaries.

Less than thirty years later, Bishop Collier found it necessary to do further work on St Mary's. Turrets had to be repaired and a leaking roof overhauled. Mosaic work and painting were done on the sanctuary and side chapels, pitch pine seats were put in the aisles and transepts, an altar was erected to the Little Flower, the organ was remodelled at a cost of £2,500, and choir stalls introduced. The cost came to £28,000 and was raised by collections throughout the diocese.

During Bishop Birch's time, the cathedral was modernised to bring it into line with the requirements of Vatican II. Under the great tower was placed a new high altar of polished limestone surrounded by copper reliefs depicting scenes of Church life in Ossory. Many other changes were made, including a new tabernacle to facilitate exposition of the Blessed Sacrament and a new organ, constructed by a distinguished German organ-builder.

St Mary's Cathedral still dominates the landscape of Kilkenny. It stands as a reminder of the faith and growing confidence of a far-off generation.

Ossory

The Rothe Monstrance

The Rothe monstrance is a very early example of the 'sunburst' monstrance. David Rothe had it made in 1644 for use in St Canice's Cathedral. Silver gilt and 59 cm in height, it was used during the Confederation period, when the city was to witness grand liturgical ceremonies, especially after the arrival of Archbishop Rinuccini. The central lunette is surrounded by small rays, while the outer ring has a flamboyant, radiant decoration. This ring has a quotation from Rev 21:3 on the front: *ecce tabernaculum Dei cum hominibus et habitabit cum eis.* And on the reverse: *ipsi populus eius erunt. et ipse Deus cum eis erit eorum Deus. Apocal. C.21.* The base has the inscription: *'DAVID ROTH EPISCOP OSSORIEN. ME FIERI FECIT ANO. 1644. ORA PRO CLERO ET POPULO DIOCESSIS OSSORIEN.'*

After the death of Bishop Rothe, the monstrance was kept in his family and later passed to the Bryan family, who presented it to St Mary's Cathedral in 1857.

Diocese of
Ossory

HISTORY OF THE DIOCESE

THE COMING of Christianity to Ossory is associated with St Kieran of Saighir, the 'first-born of the saints of Ireland' (*Promogenitus Sanctorum Hiberniae*). His foundation at Saighir Kieran flourished for many centuries. Not far away in Aghaboe, St Canice founded a monastery in the sixth century which grew in importance, giving Feargal to the church of Salzburg and eventually becoming for a time the site of the bishop's see.

The diocese of Ossory, 'Ireland's oldest bishopric', was probably coterminous with the ancient kingdom of Ossory. Its present boundaries were set at the Synod of Rathbreasail in 1111. It includes most of the county of Kilkenny (except for the parishes of Graiguenamanagh and Paulstown), part of Co Laois and the 'island' parish of Seir Kieran in Co Offaly. For a time in the thirteenth century its boundaries extended as far as the Barrow and included Graiguenamanagh.

Already before the arrival of the Anglo-Normans the winds of change had been blowing from continental Europe. The coming of the Cistercians to Jerpoint, probably around 1160, and to Kilkenny had already signalled the passing of the old Celtic order, and soon the Canons Regular of St Augustine were firmly installed in Saighir Kieran and Fertagh and had set up new foundations in Aghmacart, St John's, Kilkenny, Kells and Inistioge; their sisters were in the nunnery of Kilculiheen.

The transfer of the cathedral from Aghaboe to Kilkenny in the last decade of the twelfth century, the foundation of a cathedral chapter and the establishment of a parish system through the system of tithes introduced by the Anglo-Normans, radically transformed the ecclesiastical organisation of the diocese. More than half of the new parishes were in the hands of the religious, while the rest were run by the secular clergy – mostly the dean and chapter of St Canice's. A few were in the hands of lay patrons. In the thirteenth century the Dominicans came

to Aghaboe, the Black Abbey in Kilkenny and Rosbercon. Because of their importance in the diocese, the suppression of the monasteries in the wake of the Reformation led to enormous changes.

It was only at the beginning of the seventeenth century with the arrival of an increasing number of priests from the continental colleges and the appointment of David Rothe first as vicar apostolic and then as bishop (1618-50) that the Church began to reorganise. Rothe was the most prominent bishop in Ireland – at one stage he was the only bishop in the country – and he took a leading role in this renewal, as well as publishing a number of important works. In Ossory the old civil parishes were reorganised into twenty-nine or thirty unions, clerical conferences were introduced, confraternities established, and ecclesiastical legislation was updated. Rothe's prominence in the country and the relatively peaceful state of Kilkenny led to the Confederate 'parliament' meeting in the city in the 1640s. That period saw a flowering of religious and political activity in Kilkenny, particularly during the stay of Archbishop Rinuccini, the Papal Nuncio. The Cromwellian invasion led to a period of great difficulty for the Church, with the poet-priest Bernard Fitzpatrick, who was vicar general, martyred in 1653 and others forced to flee.

James Phelan's episcopacy (1669-95) was a period of renewal. The number of priests increased, diocesan synods were held regularly, chapels were built or restored, and the people were able to worship in relative safety. Protected by the Butler web of contacts, Phelan ordained almost one-eighth of the priests of Ireland on the 1704 list during his twenty-seven-year episcopacy, more than any other bishop in the country.

The passing of the act of 1697 saw the exile of Bishop Daton and many regular clergy, but some priests remained, and the registration of 1704 meant that they could serve their flocks in relative peace apart from a few years around 1714. New chapels were constructed and, apart

from another brief period of difficulty in the 1740s, the Church slowly recovered. As the population increased in the latter half of the century, the need to divide the large parishes was felt and extra priests were required. It was really in the first half of the nineteenth century that most of the large parishes were divided and that the situation that obtains today was largely reached. The eighteenth century saw three Dominican bishops in Ossory, two of whom were significant figures on the Irish stage – Thomas De Burgo who wrote *Hibernia Dominicana* and John Thomas Troy who later became Archbishop of Dublin.

The last quarter of the eighteenth century saw the level of tolerance towards Catholics gradually improve, and with the passing of the Relief Act of 1782, which enabled Catholics to found schools, a turning point was reached. The diocesan school that was founded in Kilkenny was the first of its kind in the country. Its motto, 'Hiems transiit', reflects this moment. Two years later, schools for the education of poor boys and girls were founded in the city. By the 1790s, upheaval on the Continent led to the need for the provision of education for priests at home, and in 1792 the college opened its doors to students of philosophy and theology, the first college in Ireland to do so. The Presentation Sisters arrived at the end of the century and soon afterwards the Christian Brothers – both providing education for those who could not afford it. The many churches built or renovated in the 1790s reflected the changing position of the Catholic community. The winter indeed had passed.

The early part of the nineteenth century saw the clergy of Ossory, led by Richard O'Donnell, oppose the Veto and support O'Connell. Bishop Marum succeeded the pious Bishop Lanigan, and he in turn was succeeded by a Carlow man, William Kinsella. Church building continued apace between 1811 and 1845, with the new St Kieran's College, a number of new parochial churches and the beginning of a new cathedral (1843) making a definite statement about the growing self-confidence of the Catholic community. Bishop Edmond Walsh oversaw the completion of St Mary's Cathedral and consecrated it in 1857. The year 1849 saw the founding of the Callan Tenant Protection Society by two curates in Callan. It was a society that was eventually to have a profound effect on the land agitation in the country.

The 'Callan Case' achieved great notoriety both at home and abroad between 1868 and 1875 as Robert O'Keeffe, the parish priest of Callan, Bishop Walsh, his successor Patrick Francis Moran (1872-84) and Cardinal Cullen became involved in civil court proceedings. Moran made a notable contribution to many areas of life in the diocese during his twelve-year stay in Ossory – local ecclesiastical history, liturgical reform, the renovation of churches, the addition to St Kieran's. Ashlin was his trusted architect. Moran was heavily involved in education on a national and local level. He brought the Mercy Sisters to Callan, the Sisters of Charity to Kilkenny and the Sacred Heart of Mary Sisters to Ferrybank. He became Archbishop of Sydney in 1884 and Australia's first cardinal the following year. He also found time to publish an edition of Archdall's *Monasticon Hibernicum*, his three-volume *Spicilegium Ossoriense* and David Rothe's *Analecta*. The clergy were already quite involved in political life at that time and were to become more involved in the land question and later still in the co-operative movement – a largely unwritten chapter in their history.

The diocese had only three bishops between 1884 and 1981 – Abraham Brownrigg, Patrick Collier and Peter Birch. Bishop Brownrigg made additions to the cathedral, brought the St John of God Sisters to the diocese and promoted Canon Carrigan's work on the history of the diocese, which eventually bore fruit in 1905 with the publication of a four-volume history of unrivaled value. During Patrick Collier's time, work continued on St Mary's Cathedral and a number of churches were built and renovated. Peter Birch, bishop in the heady days after the Vatican Council, oversaw changes in the liturgy and in the churches themselves. It was a period of great change and adaptation, not just for the Church but for society in general. Much work was done in Ossory for those afflicted by poverty and suffering from disability, work that saw Bishop Birch achieve national prominence.

St Kieran's Well, Clareen, Birr

The suspension of the seminary in St Kieran's College in 1994 marked a watershed in the history of St Kieran's and of the diocese. But the college continues to have an active role in adult religious education and formation through CREIDIM and the Maynooth Outreach Programme.

The coat of arms of the diocese has a representation of St Kieran between two pillars. It appears on episcopal arms from the eighteenth century and on a beautiful book plate of Archbishop Troy.

PLACE OF PILGRIMAGE

'Pattern' sites in the diocese

The 'pattern' or feast of the patron saint of an area was once an integral part of popular religious practice in every parish. An ancient institution, it was associated with holy wells and cemeteries, and usually included Mass. It was a great festive occasion. One of the best-known patterns was that of St John's Well on 24 June, which attracted people in great numbers from far and near. In the second half of the eighteenth century, various edicts were issued, designed to distance the Church from these occasions, which were frequently marked by faction-fighting and intemperance. The patterns continued into the following century and the demise of many only came in the quarter century or so before the Famine. Some survived and a number were renewed, albeit in a different form, later in the nineteenth century and even in recent years.

One of the oldest patterns in the diocese is that of St Moling at Mullinakill. Suspended in 1867, it was revived not long afterwards and is still celebrated annually on the first Sunday after 20 August, the feast of St Bernard. The ceremonies are ancient – the taking up of a stone from the stream feeding the well and leaving it on the altar (symbolising the leaving behind of a burden), doing rounds of the well, stopping at various stations, saying prescribed prayers, including the Rosary. By the well is an ancient alder tree from which people take twigs as a protection against fire and shipwreck.

Other places of pilgrimage include Lady Well in the parish of Ballyragget, which has increased in popularity over recent years. The pattern falls on 15 August and people come there until 8 September for various devotions, which include Mass and the Rosary. St Fiacre's well is a celebrated holy well where public devotions were carried out up to the early part of the nineteenth century and which has been revived in recent years.

Seir Kieran is perhaps the most important pilgrimage site in the diocese. It celebrates the patron of the diocese on 5 March, which is a day of special devotion for the people of the locality. The procession is the highlight of the celebration. After Mass everybody goes from the church to St Kieran's Well, around which two decades of the Rosary are recited. The well is blessed and all drink from its waters. The next station is St Kieran's Bush, where the Rosary is continued, and the last is the monastic site, where the final decade is said and a hymn sung. During the octave people continue to visit the well, reciting the Rosary and making the rounds. The climax of the celebrations is reached on the Sunday after the feast, when crowds come to follow the processional route and recite the Rosary. The pattern at Kennyswell in Kilkenny city has been revived even more recently.

Diocese of
Raphoe

Most Rev Philip Boyce DD

Bishop Philip Boyce comes from Downings, Co Donegal. He was born on 25 January 1940. Educated at Derryhassen school in Meevagh (Downings) parish and at Castlemartyr College, Co Cork, he joined the noviciate of the Discalced Carmelites in Loughrea, Co Galway, making his first profession in 1959.

Having completed philosophical studies in Dublin, he studied theology at the Teresianum in Rome, where he was ordained on 17 April 1966. He received a Doctorate in Divinity in 1974, with a dissertation on the spirituality of Cardinal John Henry Newman.

During his twenty years on the staff of the Pontifical Theological Faculty of the Carmelites in Rome (the Teresianum), he taught spirituality and dogmatic theology, and for many years was engaged in the work of the formation of students preparing for the priesthood or doing postgraduate studies.

He has been a consultor of the Congregation for the Causes of Saints since 1985, and has collaborated with the 'Centre of Newman Friends' in Rome since 1975.

Dr Boyce was ordained Bishop of Raphoe on 1 October 1995 in Letterkenny cathedral. His Motto 'In the Service of Mother Church' is of Carmelite origin. It sums up the mission he sees entrusted to him in the episcopal ministry: one of service to the People of God in the Diocese of Raphoe and to the whole Family of the Church, the Mystical Body of Christ.

He is a member of various episcopal commissions. In May 1999, the Holy Father appointed him member of the Congregation for Divine Worship and the Discipline of the Sacraments.

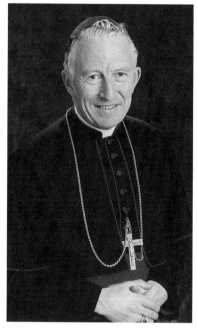

St Eunan's Cathedral, Letterkenny

The old cathedral of Raphoe passed into Protestant hands at the Reformation. In the eighteenth century the Catholic bishops came to live in Letterkenny. A church was built circa 1820 and, having been extended by Bishop Patrick McGettigan, was used as a pro-cathedral. Bishop McDevitt (1871-9) thought of building a new cathedral, and Lord Southwell promised a site, but it was not until 1891, when Bishop O'Donnell was in office, that actual building began. The cathedral was completed in 1901. Besides overseeing the cathedral project, Bishop O'Donnell had the task of providing a house for the bishop and priests of the cathedral parish.

The main benefactors were Fr J. D. McGarvey PP, Killygarvan, and Mr Neil Gillen of Airdrie. Various priests of the diocese spent considerable time fund-raising in Britain, the US and Canada.

The style is Gothic, with some Hiberno-Romanesque features, and the building is of white Mountcharles sandstone. The cathedral dominates the Letterkenny skyline. Among the artistic features to be noted are the 'Drumceat' window, by Michael Healy (North Transept); the pulpit, by Messrs Pearse (Patrick Pearse's family); the Great Arch, with its St Columba and St Eunan columns; and, outside, the fine statue of Bishop O'Donnell, by Doyle of Chelsea.

Remodelling of the cathedral took place in 1985, with the addition of an altar table and chairs; great care was taken to preserve the style and materials of the original altar. Bishop Hegarty promoted this tasteful restoration work, which left intact the architectural character of the building.

Raphoe

The Pulpit of the Four Masters

The Pulpit of the Four Masters is the work of the Dublin firm of Pearse (founded by Patrick Pearse's father). In the words of Bishop O'Donnell: 'The pulpit of the Donegal Masters, largely paid for by the National Teachers of Donegal, is a beautiful object…. What strikes one at once is the variety of materials and the exquisite workmanship. In the main, Sicilian marble is used, even in the work of the wonderfully delicate canopies that overhang the figures. But the bases are, first, granite and then Connemara, the shafts Connemara and Middleton, and the statues Carrara. The statues number ten in all; the Five Masters (for there were Four plus one), the Four Evangelists and Isaiah the Prophet. We are familiar with the richness of the Connemara green. One cannot fail to notice the wondrous lustre of the Middleton marble in this pulpit'.

The Transepts

St Eunan's Cathedral contains a unique treasure of high-quality Irish stained glass, all commissioned and executed within a few years. The North Transept is dominated by the 'Drumceat' rose window (1910) by Michael Healy (see Michael Wynne's *Irish Stained Glass*, Irish Heritage Series, no. 1).

Letterkenny was extremely fortunate to have, in Bishop O'Donnell, a pastor of foresight who engaged artists like Michael Healy to add lustre to the cathedral. This huge window depicts scenes from the life of St Columba. At the bottom of the window, we see him pleading for the bards at the Convention of Drumceat in AD 575, which took place near the present Limavady in Co Derry. King Aedh, son of Ainmire, endeavoured to banish the bards from Ireland, since 'their numbers had become excessive, and their exactions most oppressive' (M. C. Ferguson, *The Irish before the Conquest*), but Columba persuaded the king merely to reduce their numbers, not to banish them. The window also refers to Eunan's part in the controversies concerning the date of Easter.

Diocese of
Raphoe

HISTORY OF THE DIOCESE

ST PATRICK, if tradition is to be trusted, set up some bishops in Tír Conaill (Donegal), for example, his disciple, Assicus at Racoo (Drumhome parish) and Brugach in Raymochy (Drumoghill parish). Raymochy was, it seems, ruled by bishops until the eighth century, when Raphoe became the episcopal seat. But abbots now overshadowed bishops. The Iona confederacy, founded by a prince of Tír Conaill, Columba (Colum Cille, d. 597), included amongst its Irish houses such monasteries as Drumhome, Raphoe, Tory and Gartan. Adomnán (Eunan), ninth abbot of Iona (d. 704), great administrator, author, scripture scholar and legislator, was Colum Cille's kinsman.

In the twelfth-century diocesan reorganisation, the diocese of Tír Conaill had its seat at Raphoe. The Columban tradition remained vigorous at Derry, but by the thirteenth century Derry had become the seat of the northern Tír Eóghain diocese, appropriating from Raphoe Derry itself and the Inishowen penninsula. One of the new monastic orders, the Cistercians, made a foundation at Assaroe on the Erne (c. 1184). In the fifteenth century the strong Franciscan reform movement took root in the diocese, with houses at Balleghan, Magherabeg and elsewhere. Donegal 'Abbey' was the leading friary in the north of Ireland. The Carmelite friary at Rathmullan was part of this religious reform movement. The final conquest of Ulster by England (1603) made possible the introduction of the Protestant reform. The best lands were now parcelled out among English and Scottish planters, while Catholicism was proscribed. Among Catholic martyrs are reckoned in 1584 Glaisne O'Cullenan (Ballyshannon), O Cist, abbot of Boyle, and in 1612 Conor O'Devanney (Glenfin) OFM, Bishop of Down and Connor. Philip Clery, a young priest, reputedly martyred, was nephew of Abbot

O'Cullenan, whose brother, John, Bishop of Raphoe, was driven into exile in 1653.

Reconstruction after the penal night was slow. In 1704 Raphoe had fifteen registered priests, in 1731 it had for churches only five poor cabins. This was the era of the Mass Rock. Bishop James O'Gallagher (1725-37) wrote his famous *Sermons*, which for generations helped to sustain the faith and devotion of Irish Catholics. But at a time of persecution, in which at least two priests lost their lives, he was forced to leave for Kildare.

Better times came. Bishop Anthony Coyle (1782-1801) also wrote prose and poetry for popular consumption and started a little school for boys. Bishop Patrick McGettigan (1820-61) welcomed the National Schools, gave his Letterkenny house to the Loreto Sisters, and became a folk-hero for his struggle with proselytisers. His successor, Bishop Daniel McGettigan, brought the Mercy Sisters from Kinsale to Ballyshannon, before being transferred in 1820 to Armagh. He was followed in succession by Bishops Logue and O'Donnell, who became cardinals. In their day, priests like John Doherty (Gweedore) and James McFadden (Gweedore and Glenties) were prominent in the struggle to improve the lot of a people living in poverty. O'Donnell built Letterkenny Cathedral (1901), the present Bishop's House, St Eunan's College and much more. Bishop Mc Neely (1923-63) brought the Franciscans back to Ards (Capuchins) and Rossnowlagh, while Bishop Mc Feely (1965-82) had the task of implementing the decrees of Vatican II. Bishop Hegarty (1982-94) and Bishop Boyce (b. 1995) have had to meet the challenges of a rapidly changing Ireland.

PLACE OF PILGRIMAGE

Glencolumcille

Raphoe has a number of centres of pilgrimage or *turas*, for example, Doon Well, Gartan and Iniskeel. One of the oldest is that in which the pilgrim performs the devotions and recites the prayers at each of the fifteen 'stations' that circle the glen or valley of Glencolumcille. The *turas* is performed, usually on 9 June, St Columcille's feastday (although not necessarily limited to that day), and takes three to four hours. Some devout people perform the stations on three successive Fridays.

The pilgrimage, performed barefoot, is thought to date to the eighth/ninth century. The pilgrim circles each station sunwise (*deiseal*) three times, saying (usually in Irish) The Creed, Our Father and Hail Mary at each. At Station Three (Áit na nGlún), the pilgrim kneels and passes a stone around his/her body, invoking the Holy Trinity; at Station Five (Columcille's Chapel) he/she lies down on Colum's Bed, turning around *deiseal*; and at Station Seven (Columcille Well) the pilgrim drinks from the well, again in the name of the Trinity.

Standing stone, Station of the Cross near Glencolumcille

Diocese of Waterford and Lismore

Most Rev William Lee DD

William Lee was born in Newport, Co Tipperary on 2 December 1941, the eldest of five children. He received his early education at the local Convent of Mercy and Boys' National Schools and later at Rockwell College, Cashel. He studied for the priesthood at St Patrick's College, Maynooth, and was ordained on 19 June 1966. He then did postgraduate studies in Canon Law at Maynooth, receiving a doctorate in 1969. From 1969 to 1971 he served in the large parish of Finglas West, Dublin. He also studied for some time at the Gregorian University, Rome.

In 1971 he was appointed Professor of Philosophy and Bursar at St Patrick's College, Thurles, and he was President of the college from 1987 to 1993.

He served as Director of the Catholic Marriage Advisory Council (now Accord) in the Diocese of Cashel and Emly for fifteen years, and was President of Accord from 1994 to 1998. He also served on the Cork Regional Marriage Tribunal. He was ordained Bishop of Waterford and Lismore on 25 July 1993. In 1998 he was appointed Secretary of the Irish Episcopal Conference.

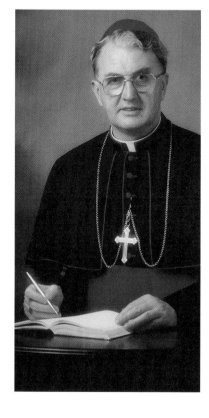

Cathedral of the Most Holy Trinity, Waterford

The Cathedral of the Most Holy Trinity, Barronstrand Street, Waterford is the oldest Roman Catholic cathedral in Ireland. The work began in 1793 with the Protestant Waterford man, John Roberts, as architect. Roberts also designed the Church of Ireland cathedral.

Over the years, additions and alterations have been made. Most of the present sanctuary was added in the 1830s; the apse and a main altar in 1854. The beautiful baldachin, which is supported by five Corinthian columns, was erected in 1881.

The carved oak Baroque pulpit, the chapter stalls and bishop's chair, designed by Goldie and Sons of London and carved by Buisine and Sons of Lille, were installed in 1883.

The stained-glass windows, mainly by Meyer of Munich, were installed between 1883 and 1888.

The Stations of the Cross, which are attached to the columns in the cathedral, are nineteenth-century paintings by Alcan of Paris. The cut-stone front was built in 1892-93 for the centenary of the cathedral.

In 1977, a new wooden altar was placed in the redesigned sanctuary. The Belgian walnut panels of the base of the altar were originally part of the altar rails at St Carthage's Church, Lismore.

There are many plaques in the cathedral. One of them commemorates fifteen famous Waterford men: Luke Wadding OFM; Peter Lombard; Patrick Comerford OSA; James White; Michael Wadding SJ; Peter Wadding SJ; Thomas White; Paul Sherlock SJ; Ambrose Wadding SJ; Geoffrey Keating; Luke Wadding SJ; Stephen White SJ; Thomas White SJ and Bonaventure Barron OFM.

Ten Waterford Crystal chandeliers were presented by Waterford Crystal in 1979.

In 1993 the Bicentenary of the Cathedral was celebrated.

The Lismore Crozier

The Lismore Crozier, together with the *Book of Lismore*, was found walled up in an ancient doorway during renovations in Lismore Castle in 1815. The bronze crozier, only 3 feet 4 inches in length, dates from the late eleventh or early twelfth century. A Latin inscription on it tells us that it was made for Niall Mac Aeducain, Bishop of Lismore (1090-1113), by the craftsman Nechtan.

The crozier can be seen at the National Museum of Ireland.

Diocese of
Waterford & Lismore

HISTORY OF THE DIOCESE

As in the case of most Irish dioceses, the origins of the Church in the Diocese of Waterford and Lismore are mainly monastic.

In the early twelfth century, when the diocesan system was coming into being, there were three ecclesiastical centres that laid claim to diocesan status: Ardmore, Lismore and Waterford. Ardmore and Lismore had monastic ancestry; Waterford had not.

Of the three centres, Ardmore was the most ancient. Its origins lay in the very early days of Christian Ireland: possibly even pre-Patrician. St Declan was its founder and his name and fame were highly revered throughout the whole territory of the 'Déise' people. Ardmore's status continued long after Declan – into the thirteenth century.

Lismore enters into Irish Church history with the arrival from Rahan in Offaly of a Kerryman named Carthach (Carthage) or Mo-chuda and his group of monks in the year AD 636. Carthach only survived one year in Lismore, but the monastery he founded was to become one of the outstanding monasteries of medieval Ireland. In the great twelfth-century ecclesiastical reform, it was particularly prominent; outstanding churchmen like Celsus of Armagh were brought to it for burial; Celsus' successor, the great Malachy, spent several years in its monastic school. Christian O'Conairce, first Abbot of Mellifont, was consecrated Bishop of Lismore in Clairvaux in 1151. He was to succeed Cardinal Paparo as Papal Legate and for nearly thirty years he was to be a very powerful Church influence in post-invasion Ireland.

The third important centre of Christianity was Waterford. Since Viking times, Waterford had become a Danish settlement and was gradually becoming Christian. The mercantile status of Waterford was second only to Dublin and, towards the end of the

eleventh century, the time seemed ripe for it to seek increased ecclesiastical importance. So a petition was sent to the Archbishop of Canterbury that a monk from Winchester be consecrated bishop for the community of Waterford. The year was 1096 and the first bishop was Malchus or, to give him his Gaelic name, Mael Isu Ua hAinmire.

And so, when the diocesan system came to be established at the Synods of Rathbreasail (1111) and Kells (1152), there were three claimants for diocesan status from the Déise region. At Kells, all three were established as dioceses. Ardmore was recognised as a diocese with its own bishop until about 1210, when it seems to have become subsumed into Lismore.

The individual dioceses of Waterford and of Lismore went their separate ways until 1363, when the Bishop of Waterford, Roger Craddock, was transferred to Llandaff in Wales, and Robert le Reve of Lismore became the first Bishop of Waterford and Lismore. And so the situation has remained ever since.

As full and accurate a list as is possible of all the Bishops of Waterford, Lismore and Ardmore is to be found on a plaque in the cathedral in Waterford. The plaque was presented to the cathedral by the priests of the diocese in 1990 to mark the episcopal silver jubilee of Bishop Michael Russell.

PLACE OF PILGRIMAGE

Ardmore

Of the many holy wells and other Christian monuments in the Diocese of Waterford and Lismore, Ardmore has to be given precedence. It is the earliest Christian site in the diocese and the oldest centre of pilgrimage. Ardmore is associated with St Declan, a very early Irish saint, quite possibly pre-Patrician. Certainly, it is very likely that the south-eastern part of Ireland would have been influenced by Christian Britain before the arrival of Patrick – and Declan may have been part of that influence.

Apart from folklore, our knowledge of Declan comes from a Life of Declan (*Vita Deglani*) preserved in a vellum manuscript in the Royal Library in Brussels. The manuscript is in the hand of Michael O'Clery, chief of the Four Masters in the late sixteenth century. The original Life, like the Lives of many of the early Irish saints, probably dates from the tenth century. Also, like those other Lives it contains many accounts of miracles and hagiographical extravagances.

The kernel facts about Declan seem to be: he was born in the Déise territory but travelled a great deal – to Britain and to Rome, where he was consecrated bishop. His main scene of evangelisation was his own native part of Ireland, and his headquarters was where the town of Ardmore now stands, about five miles east of the estuary of the river Blackwater. He spent the last few years of his life in a little cell or retreat '*dísert*' on a headland overlooking the sea; as death approached he asked to be brought back to the monastic settlement, where he died and was buried.

Ardmore has, for many centuries, attracted large pilgrimages, particularly around the feast of St Declan, 24 July. The 'pattern' of Ardmore involved a vigil and an octave. The pattern is still strongly observed, and some people continue to observe the vigil.

In Ardmore there are two clusters of buildings that should command the attention of the pilgrim:

1. To the west of the town are three buildings close together: the round tower, the twelfth-century ruined cathedral, and the Beannachán or peaked Oratory of St Declan. The Beannachán is the most important building in Ardmore; it is a small stone church which is reputed to mark the grave of St Declan. The round tower is one of the finest in Ireland, although it is probably one of the later towers – perhaps dating to the end of the twelfth century. The cathedral is a fine old pile and contains a variety of styles. It marks the importance of Ardmore, even as